Praise for *On Drumming*

"JP Bouvet's enlightening new book takes a deep dive into the challenging physical and mental aspects of drumming. These unique, clear explanations and practice strategies will help any drummer play better."

— JOHN RILEY, author of *The Art of Bop Drumming*,
professor at Manhattan School of Music

"This book is both a masterclass and a masterpiece. JP is an inspired young man, and this book offers exceptional inspiration for any musician or person that is interested in unlocking their uniquely expressive creative voice. He touches on an esoteric curriculum that is vital yet missing in many disciplines."

— STEVE VAI, 3x Grammy-winning guitarist

"This book will not only make drummers better on their instruments, but it also has the potential to help shape them into even better, more self-aware, and more creative individuals, both on and off the kit."

— MATT HALPERN, drummer for Periphery

"Understanding the concepts of this book will open the door to improvising, which will give you more enjoyment in your musical and non-musical life."

— DON LOMBARDI, co-founder of DW Drums,
founder of Drum Channel

"After I quit touring with the band and sat back down at my kit, I realized that I had no idea how to play the drums outside of a band context. My improvisational skill was zero and I wanted to fix that. The concepts and strategies that JP teaches in this book (and on his website) have helped me begin to unlock this incredible skill and have allowed me to fall back in love with playing the drums."

— STEVE JOCZ, original drummer for Sum 41

"JP Bouvet's book offers a profound exploration of drumming improvisation, combining theory, psychology, and practice. By aligning psychological principles with practical exercises, Bouvet provides a path for drummers to develop fluency and autonomy in their playing, ultimately achieving a balance between technical precision and artistic freedom."

— JUAN CARLITO MENDOZA, educator,
sub for Broadway's *Lion King*

"This book prioritizes musicality over technique, emphasizing that the limbs are merely executing our inner thoughts. It will help any drummer achieve their full musical potential. Highly recommended!"

— SERGIO BELLOTTI, professor at Berklee College of Music

"In this book, JP Bouvet deftly enmeshes psychological, theoretical, and practical considerations to help drummers become better improvisers, generously offering a means to grasp what many believe to be an elusive subject."

— DAVE DICENSO, professor at Berklee College of Music

Praise from students of *JPBouvetMethod.com*

"You deserve all the credit in the world for making drumming a creative vehicle that is accessible to all. Entering flow mode has become my form of meditation."

—Brian Chiusano

"You have totally changed my life as a drummer. I am loving the JP Bouvet Method. I have never been a better drummer."

—Dave Shadlen

"I could never have improvised something for this long before I started the course."

—David Vaughan

"I've got a regular music education, but JP is offering completely different, deeper, more creative content that you wouldn't find in a normal music school."

—Tio Nunez

"The material [JP] teaches is more interesting than a lot of what is being taught drumming-wise at music colleges."

—Martin Marschall

"I have learned more with your method than when I went to university, no joke!"

—Luis Silva

"This method is a revelation!"

—Arnaud Thomasson

"The website took my ability to improvise and
increased it tenfold."

—Nicholas Haas

"For the first time in my life I can say I play the drums with
zero imposter syndrome."

—Hoang Kindo

"JP is one of the best drummers in the world. His online class
is seriously life changing for a drummer."

—Ryan Venancio

"It's the first time in years that I'm sitting on the set and I feel
confident and free."

—Stef Gillos

"I feel like I have more ideas than I've ever had at the kit and
that is really so joyous and exciting for me."

—Ricky Carlson

"I can't believe how much more expressive I am
as a drummer now."

—Boh Kotik

ON DRUMMING

The PSYCHOLOGY *and* PHILOSOPHY
of IMPROVISATION

JP BOUVET

Invitation to Connect

One of the great pleasures of my career is connecting with drummers, teachers, and musicians around the world over our shared interests. If something in this book inspires you to connect with me, I encourage you to do so.

If you are curious about collaborating on an event at your university, drum shop, or living room, or if you are curious about how my courses can be integrated into your school or teaching program, please feel encouraged to get in touch. Write to me at jp@jpbouvetmethod.com.

For my students.

Editor: Regina Alvarado
Layout Designer: Amelia Ellis
Cover Art: Timon Ducos

Copyright © 2024

ISBN: 979-8-218-52906-2

Contents

Introduction

This book will attempt to accomplish three things. First, it will lay out principles for a theory of teaching and learning improvisation on the drums. Second, it will describe the underlying psychology that makes mastering such a complex skill possible in the first place. Finally, it will provide concrete methods that help you leverage your mind's natural tendencies in order to reliably develop creative freedom on the drums.

I have been working on creating a systematic approach to learning improvisation with my students and on my educational website for years. This is partially for the simple reason that improvisation is close to my heart. The effortless flow of improvisation has always appeared to me as the whole point of drumming and the payoff of thousands of hours of practicing. My early experiences with this feeling of flow were powerful enough to make it a lifelong goal. When my students feel this for the first time, it marks the beginning of a shift in their relationship with drumming. They shift from reciting memorized patterns to exploring infinite possibilities. Being decades into that quest, and having thousands of students whose transformations support this claim, I can share that improvisation is one of those things that is worth doing for its own sake. It becomes progressively more rewarding the more you develop the skill.

The reason I have written this book, however, is that those thousands of students, coming from all sorts of backgrounds, have made it clear to me that methods for learning to improvise are hard to come by. Very few teachers attempt to teach it, let alone teach it methodically, and something like a theory for learning improvisation is nonexistent. I do not claim to have invented the best possible way of teaching improvisation, but I can say that I have created one that works and has been deeply thought through. Given the general absence of options, this is enough for me to want to share it.

The contents of this book will include the broad philosophical principles of the approach, the subjective experience of improvising, the psychology that makes it possible, the necessary conditions for practicing improvisation, specific strategies for developing it, and ways of integrating all of your drumming vocabulary together. If I succeed, you will finish reading this book with a better understanding of how your mind works and how the drums work, as well as a feeling that controlled creative freedom is not only possible, but accessible to you.

My goal is a thorough demystifying of what often gets chalked up to "channeling the muses," "letting it flow," or giving it up to a "higher power." We will learn improvisation while leaving nothing up to chance or magic. This starts with treating improvisation as a skill that does not depend on your personality or your spiritual attunement. Ironically, however, the end of our demystifying quest will show us how the above clichés are actually important and close to the truth. Turning an analytical eye to what appears to be magic, in a beautiful twist, will only end up increasing the awe that it inspires, thus keeping us simultaneously in control of our improvisation and in thrall of the magic of music.

As I have watched my students cross the threshold of fluent improvisation, I have seen that practicing, which was once a chore, becomes expansive and rewarding; mental disorganization is replaced by a feeling of competence and control; drumming becomes a form of expression and spontaneity; and playing transcriptions gives way to just playing. My small contribution to the world is to try to facilitate these transformations in you. This book might make you a better drummer. It also might make you a better student or teacher. It might even reframe how you think about the drums entirely. Regardless, I hope most of all that this book makes you fall even more deeply in love with the art of drumming.

Chapter 1

Foundational Concepts

This preparatory chapter introduces the foundational ideas of our approach. We will carry these with us throughout the book, filling in the general definitions from this chapter with greater details and concrete examples. These ideas should always be close at hand. Our first, surprisingly challenging job is defining our goal correctly so that we can create the necessary steps to achieve it.

Our Goal

When you imagine suddenly being the drummer you wish to be, you probably imagine effortlessly playing a huge variety of things. You imagine *fluent improvisation*. While there are many smaller goals along the path, this is our ultimate goal. Let's analyze these two words separately to understand them better.

Improvisation is the act of playing unfolding drumming that is not determined in advance. Even if it relies on existing vocabulary, you combine and manipulate it on the fly in ways that are novel to you. *Fluency* is what makes your improvisation coherent and useful. Anyone can improvise by randomly hitting things on the drums, but to adhere to the passing time and the math of the measure requires fluency in the language of drums.

Fluency also implies that even when you create new ideas on the fly, you do so with accuracy, ease, control, and understanding. This combination of exploring new ideas while feeling in control will seem like a paradox to some, but this is exactly the goal we must achieve in order to realize our creative potential on the drums.

Fluent improvisation is not just about playing drum solos. It is simply your familiarity with the language of drums. You will use it to play drum solos, sure, but you will also use it to compose a drum part for a song, jam with bandmates, or to simply enjoy the feeling of creative flow in the practice room. Furthermore, it is not genre-specific. No matter the type of music you love, if you bring to mind your favorite drummer, it is safe to assume that they can improvise fluently in their respective style of music, and that this is wrapped up with their unique genius for the drums.

If fluent improvisation is not one of your goals, I hope that this book convinces you that it should be. In my years of specializing in teaching improvisation, I have never met someone who, after gaining substantial freedom on the drums, decided they would rather go back to memorizing drum parts note-by-note. It is useful to have defined our goal carefully, but in order to move from our current position toward a place of greater improvisational fluency, we need a way of knowing that we are moving in the right direction.

Our Guiding Light

Our guiding light throughout this book will be the question, *What does it feel like to improvise?* In order to understand why this question is important, consider what is missing when we point to any recording of incredible playing and think, *Learning this will help me achieve fluency.*

The problem is that, when we eventually play fluently, we will not experience it from the receiving end of a speaker or screen. We will experience it from within our minds, from the position of creator, not listener. And so, what we need to ultimately imitate is not the playing itself, but the mental state that produces that playing. In order to play like our favorite drummers, we must learn to think like them. As with any big question, many smaller questions are embedded within it, and the answers to the smaller questions help us understand the big question.

Some of those smaller questions include: While in the blurry heat of improvisation, do you think in rudiments, melodies, or abstract ideas? How far ahead do you plan the next pattern? Are you consciously choosing stickings, or is everything automatic? How can I practice in a way that builds automation? Is every sticking you know an equally valid option to play next? If so, how do you remember all of the options and choose one? Can my brain handle this without exploding? These are some of the questions we are going to answer in this book. Before we try to answer any of these questions, let alone the big question, *What does it feel like to improvise?* let's examine *why* it would be useful to know the answers. The answer to this *why* question, which is at the core of any good teaching philosophy, is *to create continuity.*

Continuity

This is a short section, but a crucial concept. Continuity, in this context, is the idea that if you know what is important at the stage of mastery, you can reverse-engineer that final experience to make earlier steps as relevant and useful as possible. This helps avoid wasting time and helps form a more practical knowledge base where newer concepts elaborate upon older ones throughout the entire arc of learning. Continuity makes everything relevant to the goal. Advanced concepts will already seem familiar when you encounter them because simplified versions have already been mastered.[1] Improvisation is not something you suddenly become ready to do. The roots of improvisation take hold at early stages, and simple forms of improvisation precede more complex ones.

The Good Teacher

Making earlier steps relevant to later ones is an idea which is simple enough to understand, but it is unrealistic to expect a new or young drummer to be able to do this without help. It is no simple task to become familiar with the feeling of improvisation, reverse-engineer relevant exercises, and then lay out a years-long course of study. Fortunately, fluency can take on an infinite number of unique forms, and there is no single path toward it that everyone must take. There is no specific set of patterns that must be memorized, and no specific type of gig that must be prepared for. Instead, the goal is to gain control generally over unfolding melodies and develop the freedom to manipulate them and orchestrate them at will.

If there are infinite paths that lead to this goal, however, there are just as many that go around in circles or nowhere at all. This is why knowing what to practice is the greatest challenge of self-taught drummers. During your earliest days, virtually anything can be considered progress. Your hands need to become comfortable simply holding sticks, and your body needs to learn where different drums are, what sounds they make, and what purposes they serve. The further along you get, however, the more ways there are to tread aimlessly, and the more important it becomes to be able to identify specific objectives and ways to achieve them.

Therefore, the most indispensable feature of a Good Teacher is their awareness of what matters. A beginner student has a very hard time imagining improvisational freedom, so they have to trust that their teacher is familiar enough with that feeling to be able to chart a sensible course. The minimum requirement for being a good French teacher, for example, is not that you can recite many French words out of a dictionary, but that you are able to fluently speak French. If your drumming goal is improvisational fluency, then the same applies to your drum teacher.

Open communication is another essential feature of the teacher-student relationship. The teacher must do their best to make sure the student understands why a given topic matters and how the current exercise relates to the long-term goal. The student, on the other hand, needs to communicate what gets them fired up and what bores them because genuine interest is the engine of motivated practice. At the end of the day, sustainable progress can be maintained when this conversation leads to a balance between what excites the student and what the teacher knows ultimately matters. The Good Teacher takes what the student is most interested in and injects whatever most closely approximates what ultimately matters. Fun is had, and progress is made. Without progress, fun wanes as the student finds themself playing the same songs and patterns over and over again. Without fun, the militant enforcing of exercises that do not interest the student will succeed only in squashing the curiosity and joy that inspired the student to practice in the first place. Awareness of the end goal should be ever-present. Where it cannot be present in the student, because of age or inability to understand, it must remain present in the teacher. A Good Teacher must be expert enough to know what matters, creative enough to reverse-engineer those things and include them during earlier stages of learning, and intuitive enough to adapt them and make them fun according to each student's needs and preferences.

Generalizable Approaches

We have just spoken about continuity *in time*—between the present and future stages of one's drumming. We can also think of continuity as moving in a lateral sense. This becomes a question of how well a method or concept *generalizes*—or, the extent to which a method or concept is able to be useful in various settings; its versatility of usefulness. The unfriendly eight-syllable word, generalizability, describes how well something does this.

Generalizability is another characteristic common to the Good Teacher's approach. Similar to what certain sciences call "fundamental laws," which remain constantly relevant, generalizable methods and concepts are applicable regardless of tempo, style, and other factors. For example, a method for gaining hand independence over a repeating foot pattern is generalizable if it can be used to gain freedom over many repeating foot patterns. A conceptual tool that helps you shape a solo is generalizable if it works just as well for a free jazz solo as it does for a punk rock one.

Although generalizability helps simplify our lives and expedite our progress, it also has its limits. It is not possible to reduce something as complex and varied as drumming into a handful of perfectly reliable protocols. Every topic offers unique problems that require unique solutions, but being able to approach a new challenge with a time-tested plan-of-attack is extremely useful. For example, if a completely different approach were necessary every time you wanted to learn to play in a new time signature, then engaging with a new time signature would be too intimidating. Instead, if you understand a series of basic steps that serve as a generally good guide when approaching a new time signature (such as: learn a few typical grooves, then work on kick drum freedom, then explore backbeat options, then think about ghost notes, etc.), then you will find yourself entering new territory with something like a map.

Because generalizable methods make you more self-reliant, you will also find yourself feeling a greater sense of ownership over your drumming because you develop the autonomy to explore new areas of drumming without step-by-step instruction. This naturally leads to the development of vocabulary that is unique to you, your ear, and your version of the process. To build this learning into lessons, I often ask students before we take a new step, "What will I ask you to do next?" As a result, they eventually start to think like me, their teacher, and thus lead their own learning, at which point my job changes to addressing the challenges that are truly unique to the topic at hand. We can summarize the role of generalizability by saying that generalizable concepts and approaches serve as rough road maps that get you far enough to encounter the nuances of the topic at hand.

A lack of generalizability is a danger not only for those skimming through videos online, but also for schools who rely on a constant rotation of guest teachers. Although this can offer a unique opportunity to see how different teachers conceptualize the same problem, in practice this is rarely possible because the school generally tries to avoid different teachers covering the same topics. The result is something like going to college and attending one lecture of a different class every day. You are likely to amass a collection of isolated facts without any analytical tools for furthering your independent study.

Without learning fundamental principles and making them relevant to something you are genuinely interested in, all of those lessons are likely to turn into one mostly-forgotten mush of half-learned ideas, accompanied by a frustrating feeling that you have spent hours watching masterclasses without actually learning anything.

As drummers, we are in particular danger of amassing disconnected tidbits because the teaching of "rhythmic theory" is not standardized in the way that harmonic theory is. For harmonic and melodic instrumentalists studying Western music using the 12-tone scale, basic classes in harmonic theory, ear training, and arranging will be remarkably similar regardless of where you study them. You spend years learning specific strategies for creating chord progressions and melodies that are effective and technically correct, but this is not the case with rhythm. You learn how rhythmic notation functions at a basic level, but you are unlikely to learn any strategies for making "rhythmic progressions," let alone making them on the fly. Besides the fact that many drum teachers tend to teach similar rudiments and use the same classic drum books, drum teachers are on their own to devise ways of conceptualizing and teaching rhythmic theory. This offers a major challenge for creating a shared conceptual framework for thinking about rhythms, and it helps explain why so many drummers feel that they lack a coherent mental framework with which to think about the drums. It also helps explain why, as we will see in the next chapter, the arsenal of rhythms that most drummers are comfortable using is surprisingly scattershot and unsystematic. At the very least, this lack of standardization increases our danger of collecting fragments of rhythmic understanding that are not connected to a reliable theory, which in turn threatens to leave us feeling like we still do not understand our instrument deeply even after decades of drumming. Part of the goal of this book is to offer basic principles for just such a rhythmic theory that applies specifically to the drum set.

The Importance of Context

The final component of this preparatory chapter is the importance of context. As often as possible, ideas should be practiced in the context of expression where they will be used. For example, when learning a language, as soon as you learn new vocabulary, you roleplay the situation where you will use it in real life. After learning taxi-related vocabulary, you pretend to take a taxi a dozen times with your teacher, who varies their responses so that you learn to respond and adapt within a context that imitates real conversation.

The problem is, drumming vocabulary is often practiced solely in an exercise context, and seldom in an improvisational context. This is the equivalent of memorizing many French words but never practicing using them in mock conversation, which prevents fluency because speaking a sentence feels different than speaking each individual word. Furthermore, if you only memorize individual words, you are more likely to forget them because it is in the context of conversation (or improvisation) where vocabulary acquires personal meaning and cements itself in memory.

If we do not practice new vocabulary in the context where we hope to use it, then what we actually acquire is a list of technical exercises that can be recited in isolation until we forget them. How many of us have played paradiddles on a practice pad for years and still not found a use for them on the drum set? Will practicing them on a practice pad for another ten years reveal something new about their utility in drum set improvisation? If instead you had never purchased a practice pad and began learning paradiddles from day one on the drum set and in ways that would later be useful in improvisation, you would not face the persistent problem that plagues many drummers—figuring out how to make rudiments, which are supposed to be the building blocks of drumming, useful on the drum set. What a strange problem.

The fact that this is a common complaint means we are missing something important. It is the step where we practice our vocabulary in a context that approximates our final setting—fluent improvisation. We will learn that this does not mean aimlessly "just playing" and trying to mix new vocabulary with everything else you can play all at once, but systematically creating a series of exercises that allows progressively more improvisational freedom as you go, starting from a place of almost no freedom at all. The important thing to remember is that playing exercises does not suddenly translate into being able to improvise. Practicing on a practice pad has its distinct benefits, but the point here is that rudiments do not become useful merely because you can play them. Similarly, being able to make free throws on your driveway does not make you a good basketball player. You have to be able to make shots *in the game.*

Creativity Doesn't Matter

You might be feeling some insecurity as we get into the meat of this book, thinking, *Do I have what it takes to become a fluent improviser? Am I sufficiently creative?* To alleviate this doubt, one thing that this book will thoroughly demonstrate is that improvisation is a skill, not a gift.

Different people have natural knacks for different things, but I can tell you with utmost certainty that you are more than capable. The methods in this book are designed to leverage fundamental features of the human mind that we all share. Improvisation does not depend on you being creative, artsy, or any other personality type, so we can discard from the beginning the mushy, unhelpful concept of creativity.

What we really mean when we say that we want to *feel creative* on the drums is that we want to have options—a lot of options. So many options that we no longer feel like we are even choosing between options, but instead acting as guides to a feeling of freedom in which the limbs obey the mind and even provide pleasant surprises from time to time. We want to sit down at the drums, open a faucet of ideas, manipulate them along the way, feel in control, and actually like the sound. We want fluent improvisation. I have had students who are among the most naturally uncoordinated people I have ever met, and I have watched them use the principles and methods in this book to patiently build the skill of improvisation to an impressive and personally rewarding degree. You can too. I will occasionally use the word creative because it is a useful adjective, but I am never referring to it as an innate gift.

Conclusion

We have just laid out the principles of our budding philosophy of drum set improvisation. This is what is required for learning improvisation at the most general level. To review, these principles are as follows:

1) *The feeling of improvisation* helps us understand what internal tools we need to develop.
2) Early steps should be relevant to the end goal to form continuity.
3) The value of a Good Teacher is in their knowledge of what matters and their ability to adapt it to the interests of the student.
4) Generalizable approaches expedite our progress and make us more self-reliant.
5) New vocabulary must be practiced in an improvisational context if we hope to use it during improvisation.
6) Creativity does not matter because improvisation is a skill, not a gift.

Let's continue by pursuing a deeper understanding of our guiding light, moving from broad principles to the subjective experience. As continuity has shown us, if we are going to create a successful approach to learning to improvise, we need to understand some key features of what it feels like to be fluent.

Chapter Terms

- **Improvisation**: Unfolding drumming that is not determined in advance.

- **Fluency**: Improvisation done with accuracy, ease, control, and understanding.

- **Fluent Improvisation**: Our goal. A skill that anyone can develop.

- **The Good Teacher**: Makes continuity possible because they know what matters. Uses generalizable approaches Mixes interests of students with what matters.

- **Continuity**: When early steps imitate later steps and mastery. Expedites progress and prevents wasting time.

- **Generalizability**: How well a concept or approach works in multiple different contexts. Expedites progress and encourages self-reliance.

Chapter 2

What It Feels Like to Improvise

The previous chapter gave us a guiding light, broad principles for our approach, and a good reason for following them. In this chapter, we will examine that guiding light—what it feels like to improvise—more closely. Most people assume that it feels like effortless flow, but that is not enough. We need to define key features of the experience so that, with the principle of continuity in mind, we can reverse engineer them and make early exercises as relevant and useful as possible. If improvisation is a skill, then we need a way of paving our path to it by first encountering rote drills, then proto-improvisational exercises, then highly-constrained improvisational exercises, and eventually full improvisation. If we succeed in creating continuity at each of these stages, then each will prepare you with early versions of the physical and mental tools that you will actually use when you attain fluency. What we learn about the subjective experience of improvisation in this chapter will directly impact the exercises and strategies that we create throughout the rest of the book.

The Creative Director

I like to relate the mental experience of improvising to the job of a Creative Director. Fluent improvisation feels like overseeing and managing a task as it unfolds. A Creative Director is primarily concerned with the vision, the general direction, and the aesthetic, but they also have to make sure the members of the team (in a drummer's case, their limbs) are well-coordinated. Although the Creative Director's primary viewpoint is from a "higher" perspective, they occasionally need to get their hands dirty in the details as well, intervening in the technical work of fixing errors or offering specific guidance to a team member during a challenging task. When drumming, you want to spend most of your time listening and reacting, but you will frequently need to drop all of that higher-level oversight to make sure that a pattern gets executed correctly.

Focal Distance

The idea of the Creative Director goes hand-in-hand with another borrowed concept: focal distance. In photography, you can zoom in the lens of your camera and bring all of your vision to bear on the minute details of a small object to the exclusion of everything else. Conversely, you can make your vision as wide as possible by zooming all the way out and taking in the entire scene. Likewise, when you pay close attention to something, it feels subjectively like you are "zooming in" the lens of your attention, focusing narrowly on an item, feeling, or sound while everything else blurs or disappears.

In drumming, this happens when you become intensely focused on tiny details, like the mechanics of your thumb while you play the ride cymbal, or when you suddenly begin paying close attention to whether the beater is rebounding off the kick drum. This type of hyper-focus is often involuntary and can be made worse by nerves. This can distract you from the flow of playing, especially when you feel unable to zoom back out and assume your supervisory Creative Director perspective. When drummers play their first show on a drum set different from the one they are comfortable playing at home, they often become so unwillingly hyper-focused on the difference in the height of the seat or the tilt of the snare that they remain distracted for the entire show. To be stuck in this narrowly zoomed-in perspective makes it impossible to hear the music of your drumming and fellow musicians, and prevents you from making broader creative decisions. You become the Creative Director who micromanages, neglecting your job as a visionary and getting in the way of workers who you should trust to do their jobs. On the other hand, focal distance can be zoomed out too far when, for example, in the middle of a show, you are thinking about whether to order regular or sweet potato fries from the bar later. This is the Creative Director whom no one has seen in days and is not responding to emails. The work becomes aimless, and small problems, which go unanticipated, cause train-wrecks (you miss a cue, do not drop out when you are supposed to, and keep playing through the vocal break).

We all know what it feels like to be zoomed in, but many of us are not familiar with the feeling of zooming out the right amount to a supervising position because it requires achieving a certain level of automation. On the road to fluent improvisation, you will learn how to build layers of creative automation through methodical exercises that allow us to make improvisation effortless. This is what will progressively enable us to leverage the idea of focal distance, so we can avoid getting stuck too zoomed in or zoomed out.

Let's use an example to help us imagine what it will feel like to hover between these extremes. Let's say you are soloing. As a well-balanced Creative Director, you decide to throw into the mix of your improvisation a new linear pattern that you have been working on. You can consistently play the pattern in the practice room, but it requires a lot of focus because the coordination is challenging. As you start playing it, you will likely zoom in to make sure the execution goes as planned. Perhaps you know that when you play this specific pattern you need to pay attention to how your left hand lines up with your left foot at certain moments, and so your attention is absorbed with tracking this. Now, having successfully brought the new pattern into the mix, you zoom back out, listening to the melody that this new pattern creates, and make a broad general directive: *Let's make a hihat groove based on that melody from the toms.* You are not yet sure what that groove is actually going to sound like. In fact, you have automated these familiar melodies and patterns to the extent that at no point will you zoom in far enough to even notice what stickings or rudiments you end up using, but you know you have a well-trained team, and if you tell them the general direction, in this case a specific melody within your rhythmic vocabulary, they will deliver something you can work with. Delightfully, as is the case with every well-trained team with good leadership, since you are never planning the details, there is even an element of pleasant surprise at each of these transitions, as the team draws from their deep wells of experience to execute the melody in one of the infinite ways it could be orchestrated. If it seems hard to believe that this level of automation is possible, read on.

Rhythmic Vocabulary

Another defining feature of the mental experience of improvising is that it involves more or less a constant internal flow of rhythmic melodies. When I say *rhythmic melodies,* I do not mean melodies with pitches and tones like those a vocalist sings. I mean monotone or two-tone beatbox-type rhythms that roughly imitate the drum set. All of the various rhythmic melodies you can string together make up your *rhythmic vocabulary.* Rhythmic vocabulary is the root of all creative drumming, while a lack of such rhythmic options results unavoidably in drumming that is uninteresting and repetitive.

When I say that becoming a fluent improviser requires that you ultimately end up "thinking in melodies," I am not saying, and this is a crucial distinction, that you must end up thinking *about* rhythmic melodies. This distinction reveals something important about how we learn improvisation. You must think a lot *about* rhythmic melodies in order to eventually think *in* rhythmic melodies. Put another way, mastery of lower-order rhythmic vocabulary must come before higher-order conceptual thinking. As a parallel example, consider that an author, when asked about their creative process, will never say, "I am thinking about words." Words are the substance of writing. Rhythms are the substance of drumming. Just as you cannot express an idea in English without first learning many English words, you cannot express an idea in the language of drumming without being able to effortlessly produce a variety of rhythmic melodies. The master drummer is thinking with rhythms, but they are not usually thinking about rhythms. The author is thinking with words, but they are not usually thinking about words. What enables these masters to transcend the basic building blocks which make up their respective languages is that the required vocabulary has been sufficiently automated. With deep pools of vocabulary readily available, the author and improviser are able to think in higher-order ideas like motif, contrast, and narrative.

To bring all of this close to home, many drummers do not realize that they have a severe lack of rhythmic vocabulary. If I ask a student to sing a one-measure rhythm, and then I ask them to sing a different one, and I repeat this process, it is very common for students to start repeating themselves after only four or five turns. In case that does not seem problematic, what I am saying is that it is more likely than not that a drummer who has played the drums for several years has a rhythmic vocabulary that contains *only four or five rhythmic melodies.* This very same drummer might have excellent technique, be able to execute all their rudiments flawlessly, and may even make their living playing shows. If that seems difficult to believe, keep in mind that there is a difference between rhythms you can read off a page or repeat after hearing them, and rhythms that you can create from your own mind—only the latter makes up your rhythmic vocabulary.

This helps us understand one way that advice from great drummers about soloing can be very unhelpful—it often assumes that we already have a substantial rhythmic vocabulary like they do, and the advice is therefore usually abstract, conceptual, and artistic. A master drummer who has been fluent for decades can easily forget what drumming felt like before they were fluent, and can therefore give you advice that is perfectly sincere, but unhelpful. This is why there is a difference between the questions, "What are you thinking while you improvise?" and "What should I be thinking while I improvise?" If we are asking a master improviser, and we are not yet a proficient improviser ourselves, then the answers to these questions might differ greatly. To the first question, our master improviser might answer that they are thinking about telling a story. The answer to the second question, however, might be: do some highly technical exercises to expand your rhythmic vocabulary so you can begin creating interesting melodies. After you can do that, then you can start making artistic decisions about how to apply them, and then, a year from now, you can start telling a story.

If you then take this response to your private lesson teacher to ask for guidance, let's imagine a response that has continuity, and one that does not. The Good Teacher from the previous chapter might give you creative exercises that help you learn to play and understand some limited unfolding melodies that are useful for improvisation, both now and later. This will help you start to build the mental tools required for improvising and get a small taste of what improvisational fluency feels like. Conversely, a teacher that does not apply continuity, generalizability, and awareness of what matters might double down on further improving your technique, which may have never been the problem in the first place, or by having you learn a long transcription of a solo by the drummer who gave you the advice without explaining how it leads toward your goal of fluency.

Like with the hypothetical student above, chances are, if you are reading this book, that you would increase your creative potential most substantially not by utilizing a new artistic, abstract visualization technique, but by multiplying your rhythmic vocabulary *and then* experimenting with narrative ideas. In essence, contrary to much masterclass advice about soloing, I am saying that you need to think a lot *about* rhythms, ideally in a systematic way, so that you can eventually become so good at thinking about them that you begin to think *in* rhythms.

Rhythmic Stream of Consciousness

When William James coined the term *stream of consciousness*, he was observing how the mind unceasingly strings one thought to the next whether we want it to or not.[2] If you have tried meditating, you know how remarkably automatic this thought-creation process is. On the drums, the level of automaticity that we hope to develop with our rhythmic vocabulary can be thought of as a *rhythmic stream of consciousness*—a state where rhythmic melodies connect themselves in a constant, never-ending flow with such ease that you need merely open the faucet and supervise its unfolding. Unlike James' definition, however, this is something we are going to actively develop. Nothing in this approach will be left to chance. Your rhythmic stream of consciousness will be the result of developing the skill of melodic improvisation, which we will explain how to do carefully in the coming chapters. If this level of automaticity is difficult to imagine, notice the ease with which verbal thoughts flow through your mind. Rhythm is a much simpler language, so the level of automaticity required for rhythmic improvisation is certainly within your reach.

Despite the fact that we are all capable of developing a free-flowing rhythmic stream of consciousness, most drummers never arrive at this major improvisational milestone because it is almost universally overlooked in drum set learning. At some point you might have seen a video of your favorite drummer singing their drumming, or improvising by beatboxing. Even if you have not, it is impossible to imagine that your favorite drummer does not possess this ability. This is not reflective of some fine-tuned beatboxing technique, but of the simple fact that the faucet of rhythmic melodies flows from a reservoir of rhythmic vocabulary that is expansive— *the same reservoir* from which flows the ideas they deliver to the drum set. We should take this simply as a sign that our *thinking about drums* needs to advance along with our physically playing them.

To further illustrate this point, consider why the *guitarist* in my band is a more interesting drummer than most drummers. As I stated at the beginning of this section, a lack of rhythmic vocabulary is the cause of most boring drumming. It creates the feeling that you are playing the same thing over and over again, and it is rarely identified as a problem at all. My guitarist has spent a lot of time developing his rhythmic vocabulary as it applies to the guitar. However, since rhythmic vocabulary exists separate from any specific instrument, it is immediately transferable. That is why he can sit down at a drum set and, with no technique and minimal coordination, muscle out more interesting drum grooves than most drummers who have played for years.

In contrast, I regularly encounter students who can play remarkably fast, have refined technique, and might even tour with a famous band, but cannot think of an interesting melody from scratch to save their life. The truth of the matter is that no amount of technique or speed will fix your vocabulary problem. Your drumming will indeed be fast, but it will be fast and boring. Of course, this is not to say that technique and speed are not important, but for how much attention they receive compared to rhythmic vocabulary, I find that they are almost never what is preventing my students from achieving improvisational fluency.

Listening vs. Speaking Vocabulary

If rhythmic vocabulary is so essential, why does no one notice it is missing? A fact of language is that everyone understands more words than they use in conversation, and this is no different for the language of drumming. Put another way, there is a difference between your listening/reading vocabulary and your speaking vocabulary. *Predigested* is a word which I have just read in a sentence and understood without pause, but I do not believe I have ever used that word while speaking. If exactly that word was needed for me to deliver an idea, it is likely that I simply would not be able to think of it. Even if I did manage to come up with it, it would only come to me after I paused and stuttered a few times. In this case, the problem is not that I cannot recall the word if I need it, it is that the word is not readily available in the flow of conversation.

When speaking, it is normal to pause for a few seconds while recalling a word, but drumming does not allow for this. On the drums, this feeling of stuttering, often described as a feeling of short-circuiting, will feel very familiar to many drummers who despair at doing so in the middle of big fills. The reality of drumming is that if I cannot complete the sentence without pausing and stuttering to think of the right pattern, then my attempt becomes, objectively, a mistake. The word that made me stumble might be part of my listening and reading vocabulary, which means I am not confused when I hear the rhythm played by someone else, but it is not a part of my speaking vocabulary, so it does not flow out of me as I express my thoughts.

The analogy deepens when we consider that not only do I know what *predigested* means, but I know how to pronounce and spell it. This reveals something sneaky about our speaking vocabulary—it flies under the cover of our listening vocabulary. We think that if we know the sticking (spelling) of a rudiment and can play it (pronounce it) in isolation, then we are capable of using it in improvisation (conversation). To state an obvious but consequential fact, you can only use words (melodies) that come readily to mind. What does not come to mind might as well not exist. Whether you practiced a pattern for two hours or two months, if it does not appear in your rhythmic stream of consciousness, then the fact that you know that it exists does not make it part of your speaking vocabulary.

This difference between the speaking and listening vocabularies reveals itself in a very specific way with students and was the catalyst that helped me realize that rhythmic vocabulary was the central tenet of teaching improvisation. Sitting across from a student, I would sing an uncommon rhythm and ask them to repeat it. They would do so without a problem. We would do this several times. Then I would ask them to think of their own unique and uncommon rhythm, but, alas, they would not be able to. Instead, they would fall back on extremely common, habitual melodies. If they had come in saying, "I feel like I am always playing the same thing," then the nature of the problem would become immediately clear: they were stuck always playing the same melodies, but were dressing them up with different orchestrations that disguised the underlying lack of variation. They could understand and repeat complex melodic language, but they could not create it themselves.

My friend who studies Indian classical music told me that some Indian percussion gurus prioritize the development of rhythmic vocabulary to such an extent that they do not allow their students to touch an instrument for two years. During that time, the students learn only to understand, internalize, and verbalize rhythmic melodies. They are not distracted by technical exercises at the expense of what is more fundamental. The most important work gets done first, and it must be thrilling to have so much creative potential already waiting to burst forth when they first touch the instrument. I imagine that the repetitive and sometimes tedious work of developing technique, speed, and coordination is made much easier by the fact that they already know what it will enable them to do because they can already sing it. To recall the introduction of this book, before these students even touch an instrument, they already understand what fluency will feel like because they have become verbally fluent in the language of their instrument before playing a single note. It is no coincidence that Indian classical musicians are world-renowned for their prodigious improvisation.

Trying to improvise without rhythmic vocabulary is like trying to write poetry after learning only five words in a new language. Worse yet, exact imitation with no understanding of underlying rhythms is like reciting poetry in a foreign language by mimicking the sounds. If you are persistent, you might eventually learn some things by ear, but eventually, you will need to know how the language works before you can express your ideas clearly, let alone artistically.

Orchestration

If your job was to play the triangle, then rhythmic vocabulary would be all you need, but, since we play not one instrument but a collection of instruments, orchestration, along with the comparative dynamics, tone, and feel within orchestrations, is what makes the possibilities grow exponentially. As you develop ways to leave the melodic faucet running, you can direct more of your attention to adjusting the orchestration of those melodies in interesting ways. This is what you spend most of your life doing, and this is where "infinite possibilities" enter the picture. If you sing a monotone rhythm in a two-bar space, the number of melodies you can create is sizable, but limited. With a year's concerted effort, you could get to the point where all of those melodies are available to you. After that point, however, your work would have only just begun. You could now shift your attention to the infinite number of creative ways that you could orchestrate those melodies on the drum set.

Let's take a look at how changes in orchestration multiply the creative potential of your rhythmic vocabulary. Let's say you have reached the point where you can leave the melodic faucet open with little trouble. In other words, you can beatbox interesting rhythms without stopping for several minutes using some of the methods we will cover in the coming chapters. You then have the option to deliver that unfolding rhythm, for example, to the kick drum underneath an eighth-note groove, or a quarter-note or sixteenth-note groove. You might decide to add ghost notes, or reassign one of the kick notes to a snare accent, or you might do away with the backbeat altogether and let the snare take over more of the melody. You might decide to repeat a portion of the melody, or let it change. You might move your right hand to the ride, or the bell, or the crash, or the stack, or the rim, or the floor tom. You might make the dynamics really flat, or really deep. You might play it straight, or swung, or somewhere in the middle. You might fire up a samba ostinato on the feet and play the melody with flams on the toms, or play the same melody with only your right hand while the left plays ghost notes. You might play the melody on double kick underneath a halftime groove on the stack.

We could, of course, do this all day, adjusting the dials of delivery in an infinite number of ways. The multiplying effect really comes into focus when we remember that during all of these orchestration changes, the underlying melody is simultaneously also constantly evolving. This gives us two levels of improvisation happening at the same time: the melodic layer and the orchestration layer. Of course, we always have the option to freeze one or the other in place, but, in the spirit of pinning down the subjective experience of improvisation, you are ultimately going to feel these two layers of improvisation as intertwined but separate creative targets. When people feel like they are playing the same thing over and over again, it is often because, even though they are varying the orchestration in ways like I just described, they are always playing the same underlying melodies. Orchestration is important, but rhythmic vocabulary is still the root of all creative drumming.

I do not want the last couple paragraphs to give the impression that you must first do A, then do B for the rest of your life. Realistically, unless you are studying with one of the aforementioned Indian gurus, it is never that tidy. You will want to actually hit the drums on Day 1, and you should. You will start developing coordination, technique, and independence from the beginning, and you should. Most drummers do not pick up sticks for the first time and decide on the spot to commit themselves to a life of percussion, and so take the path of gurus. I certainly did not. We dabble. We try stuff out. We want to hit stuff and play along to songs. Coordination, technique, and speed matter a great deal. Playing along with songs, and just messing around matters. The point is to balance all of these things with the only essential element that is reliably neglected: your ability to generate interesting rhythms.

Flow

As we try to put the feeling of improvising into words, you might be thinking that the rhythmic stream of consciousness sounds similar to what people call a "flow state." Countless artists have shared that when they are in their purest state of creation, they do not think at all. The psychologist who first researched this phenomenon systematically and coined the term *flow* was Mihaly Csikszentmihalyi (I feel slightly less bad about *generalizability* now). As he describes it, people in a flow state become so deeply engaged in the task that they lose their sense of self-consciousness, their sense of time becomes distorted, complicated actions are executed easily and without forethought, and they find the activity intrinsically rewarding.[3] For an artist, it can feel as though you become a channel through which a higher power seems to speak. Anyone who tells you that this is the goal is absolutely correct. Being in flow is indeed a powerful creative experience. Not only do you operate as closely to your true potential as possible, but people tend to report these moments as peak experiences in life.

However, the idea of flow can be misleading. The reason that the advice, "Just don't think," is not helpful is that you cannot simply *choose* to be in flow. It is something that happens. Realistically, given the nature of our task, most of your time will not be spent in a flow state. Therefore, the advice, "Just don't think of anything when you solo," or, "Just get in the flow," is not particularly useful. In fact, it can even be counterproductive to a new drummer who could benefit from actual creative exercises but who instead never works on improvising because it is made to sound like a trance state for mystics. That is why, on the contrary, good advice on improvising helps you *think better*, in more creatively productive ways, and is designed to be useful while you remain quite aware of your existence, perhaps even a little anxious about the solo you are performing.

That said, even though we cannot choose to be in flow, awareness of how it works can help us create the conditions that make it more likely to happen, which, fortunately, are the same conditions that make your practicing as productive as possible. Flow is most likely to occur when the demands of the task are perfectly matched to the edge of your abilities. If the task is too easy, boredom ensues. If it is too hard, frustration and discouragement are likely.

There are a couple important things to keep in mind about flow. First of all, you come in and out of it. Michael Jordan was not in a state of flow every time he picked up a basketball. He was good regardless. If you think you have experienced flow, you almost certainly have. It can happen in the midst of conversation, reading a book, or exercising, and usually happens momentarily. You might experience flow for a few measures when you are playing along with music before you become aware of something that takes you out of it again. Annoyingly, it is one of those things, like "being in the moment," where once you think about being in it, you are no longer in it.

The other thing to remember about flow is that it is possible at every stage of learning, including beginning stages.

It is not about doing something superhuman. It is about the demands of the task matching the edge of your capacity, even if the task is objectively simple and your capacity limited. The implications in the practice room are that you want to create exercises that have you balancing effortfully on the edge of your comfort zone, which may seem paradoxical given how effortless flow feels when it finds you. This is also where progress is made most quickly.

This might sound like everything needs to be complicated (and exhausting), but this is not the case. What matters is not necessarily complexity, but depth of focus. Every area of study can be made deeper. This is in fact what happens quite naturally as you get better. As you learn to play more in time with the metronome, you also improve your ability to hear how off the metronome you are. In this way, you never arrive at perfection even though the errors are imperceptible to a less experienced ear. If you are going to play quarter notes and try to match the metronome, do so with intense enough concentration that you find the edge of your comfort zone even with this simple task. Whether or not this is the best use of your time is another question. Being in a flow state does not necessarily mean you are doing something useful. The difficult part of this equation is the fact that "the demands of the task" when practicing an instrument are usually self-imposed. You are not climbing a mountain, which kindly supplies the obstacles. On the drums, you (or a Good Teacher) are responsible for creating the challenge, as well as continually adjusting it to match your newly acquired skills. This meta-skill of adjusting constraints to guide your own development is going to be a major focus of further chapters because it is a hallmark of both a Good Teacher and a self-reliant student.

At the end of the day, whether or not you enter a flow state does not really matter. It is not synonymous with fun, nor excellence. Again, leaving nothing up to chance, we will prepare ourselves throughout this book to improvise well regardless. Every now and then, you will surely slip into a flow state, and then slip out of it. Most of the time, you will not notice it happened.

Conclusion

To summarize, when we try to answer the question *What does it feel like to improvise?*, we find the following:

1) Your conscious role while playing will be that of the Creative Director.

2) This experience will include a more or less constant and effortless flow of rhythmic melodies, which is a skill we will develop.

3) Much of your energy will be spent deciding how to deliver those melodies to the drum set.

4) Your focal distance will zoom in when something demands your attention, and out when things are running smoothly.

5) Sometimes you will slip into a flow state when the task at hand demands your full capacity and deep concentration.

Chapter Terms

- **Creative Director**: The role you play as you oversee your unfolding improvisation. Generally listening, reacting, directing, but sometimes intervening with execution.

- **Focal Distance**: How "zoomed in" your attention is— narrow to observe a small detail, or wide to listen and take in the whole scene. The ideal default is hovering somewhere in the middle.

- **Rhythmic Vocabulary**: The rhythms you are so familiar with that you use them without trying. Your "speaking vocabulary" on the drums. The root of all creative drumming.

- **Orchestration**: How you deliver your rhythmic vocabulary to the drum set.

- **Flow State**: A state of deep immersion resulting in loss of sense of self, dilation of time, and peak performance. Most likely when the demands of the task match the edge of your ability.

Chapter 3

Think Simple Thoughts, Play Complex Things

This is the "Psychology 101" chapter, as it pertains to the drums. To orient us, we have been moving from broad and conceptual toward specific and mechanical, and we will continue to do that. In Chapter 1, we learned what is required for success when learning an improvisational skill. In Chapter 2, we moved into the mind of the improvising drummer, speaking mostly metaphorically and conceptually, and tried to get a solid grasp of what it feels like to improvise. In this chapter, we move a level deeper than the subjective experience and learn how your mind works. This includes the different types of memory, how we consolidate complex information so it can be easily recalled, five different ways of understanding a rhythm, the nature and limits of attention, and something I call motor intuition. We will see how your mind has a remarkable ability to reduce complexity into small, manageable, consolidated units. Our success with improvising hinges on this ability because in order to improvise we need to increase the complexity of our playing while maintaining the simplicity of our thoughts. As we will see, creating this dynamic between simple thoughts and complex drumming is our only option, and is, in fact, the entire goal of practice.

Procedural and Declarative Memory

It is hard to overstate the enormous role that memory plays in learning. Without memory, the idea of learning is hard to even rationalize. Everything you know, and everything you know how to do, is stored in memory. A computer without memory is not only useless, it ceases to compute. Even a simple calculator needs to "remember" how to add and subtract the numbers you enter.

There are two different types of human memory: declarative memory and procedural memory. *Things you can tell me you know* (things you can declare) make up declarative memory. This includes things like the capital of Alaska and the sticking of a paradiddle. It can be expanded by facilitating the transfer of new information from short-term to long-term memory, for example through repetition and other methods. On the other hand, procedural memory is made up of *things you can show me you know by doing them*. This involves things you can do but would have a hard time describing with words, like juggling, buttoning a shirt, or doing a cartwheel.[4a] Improvising relies on both, but more heavily on procedural memory, so let's start by understanding how that type of memory works.

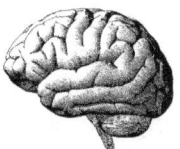

Memory

Declarative Memory	Procedural Memory
Things you can show me you know by telling me (explicit facts).	Things you can show me you know by doing them (difficult to explain).
Examples: • Capital of Alaska • Favorite hockey player • Paradiddle sticking	Examples: • Riding a bicycle • Doing a cartwheel • Playing a paradiddle

Procedural Memory

Once mastered, tasks stored in procedural memory are easy to do, but hard to explain. The classic example is riding a bike. If I asked you to explain to me how to ride a bike, once you got past "pedal" and "don't fall," there would be little else to say. Yet, riding a bike is incredibly complex, and the fact that anyone, let alone five-year-olds, can do it is miraculous. At every moment, countless complex calculations, fed by your sensory systems, based on an intuitive understanding of the laws of physics, command countless large and small muscular contractions that ideally keep you upright and moving forward. Riding a bike requires dozens of muscles to work in concert, but this coordination goes largely unnoticed.

Because of the complexity and automaticity of tasks governed by procedural memory, it tends to feel like this type of memory is stored in our muscles, not our brains. When we pay attention to it, it feels very much like the part of us that remembers how to ride a bike is down where our limbs are, which is perhaps why we call it muscle memory. However, everything your muscles do is commanded by one or multiple parts of your brain.

If we take a moment to appreciate how complex the act of advanced improvisation is, it should come as no surprise that it happens almost entirely through procedural memory. This brings up something that might seem like a paradox. *If improvisation is the act of creating new things on the spot, how can it also rely so fully on retrieving things from memory? Does that not negate the very idea of improvisation?* Perceiving this as a problem stems from being stuck thinking only of declarative memory—as a set of known, identifiable pieces of information that can be recalled. Colloquially, when we use the word memory this is usually what we mean. We say a person has a "good memory" when they remember facts and events in great detail. No one uses the word memory to describe procedural memory. We would never say Michael Jordan was the best in the game because he had a great memory, even though, by definition, his highly developed procedural memory for basketball is what made him great.

We would instead simply say Michael Jordan was really good at basketball.

When we consider that we are drawing on procedural memory when improvising, instead of declarative, the paradox disappears. When you ride a bike, you use the same senses and muscles every time, even when you are exploring a new part of town. When you turn a corner, it does not feel like you are merely recalling the "turn-a-corner factoid" from your memory bank. It feels like you are creatively navigating a turn, which feels unlike any other specific turn you have ever taken. This is also how it feels to share a thought with a friend or to improvise a two-bar fill between sections of a song—you might use the same words and patterns you often use, but the meaning or music you create on the fly is something new.

To bring us to the point of exhausting the bike metaphor, it is important to point out that, for most drummers, drumming never becomes anything like riding a bike. Not enough gets automated. Not enough gets transferred to procedural memory. We learn to ride a bike quickly because the goal is clearly defined (avoid falling over), and we receive a constant stream of feedback from physics, which provides very clear and potentially painful evidence of whether or not we are succeeding. Improvisation is less kind.[5] There is no physics of improvisation against which we measure our success. There is no "falling off" that provides corrective feedback before the next attempt. This is why many of us become stuck. The goal of subsequent chapters will be to explain how we can develop ways of practicing that serve this purpose—proto-improvisational exercises that, like training wheels on a bike, help us develop the intuition in our procedural memory and pave the path to fluency.

Declarative Memory

Declarative memory applies to drumming in different ways depending on if you are performing or practicing. During a performance, in the blurry heat of improvisation, the Creative Director generally speaks in declarative memory terms. Although the *execution* of improvisation is done by procedural memory, the *directing* of improvisation is done by declarative memory. The Creative Director resides in the office of declarative memory, and sends forth general or specific instructions to the team (limbs) who are already in the midst of executing a previous idea. The instruction might be specific, *Let's use that pattern I worked on yesterday*, or general, *Make it sound more smooth.*

In the practice room, declarative memory serves a different purpose. If improvising means moving between many options, then it implies also knowing the technical difference between similar options in declarative terms. We use declarative terms in the practice room to specify what we are currently doing *(This groove includes a kick on the 'a' of Beat 3)*, which then helps us define what other options are available *(I could play a kick on the '&' of Beat 3 instead)*. Therefore, declarative memory is where you store your understanding of how rhythms work, technically and mathematically.

Rules, exercises, methods, ostinatos, stickings, and notation are the things of declarative memory. Without understanding your drumming in declarative terms, your procedural memory, left unsupervised, will develop only a small set of repetitive habits. If you cannot identify in declarative terms what those habits are, you will be doomed to repeat them forever. For example, identifying that you habitually put a massive crash on Beat 1 after a fill (a declarative fact) could lead to a decision to practice putting a massive crash on Beat 2 instead. You might initially find that this is awkward and that you do not have the vocabulary to do so. As you find ways to develop that vocabulary on the drums, you accumulate new options, both at the declarative level *(I can now consciously choose to crash on Beat 1 or 2)* and at the procedural level *(regardless of which I choose, my "team" can execute the command)*. Furthermore, as you listen to your own playing, you identify in declarative terms what is working. Declarative and procedural memory constantly interact, work together, and influence each other.

Chunking

Now that we see how seemingly simple activities like riding a bike are actually very complex at the procedural level, it is easy to see why our brains need some way of consolidating information and unpacking it quickly when needed. One way our brains do this is by *chunking*. Chunking is the process of consolidating many pieces of information into a single "chunk" (these are the technical terms, believe it or not). You can think of a chunk as a drawer with a label. The benefit of chunking is that, once something is sufficiently "chunked," you need only recall the label of the drawer in order to automatically unpack all of the information that it contains.[4b] People usually talk about chunking in the context of expanding short-term, declarative memory (things like memorizing your bank account number). However, what we are interested in is how chunking in declarative terms slowly loads your *procedural* memory with increasingly complex drumming scripts, which it can then execute in response to simple declarative prompts. This underlies our ability to continue thinking simple thoughts while our playing becomes more complex.

First, let's understand chunking in its typical presentation. If you were sitting in an *Introduction to Psychology* class, the classic example preceding the lecture on memory would go something like this: the professor asks you to remember as many of the following letters as you can, and then reads them one after another very slowly (you cannot see them):

X N S A F B I C I A X

Once finished, you have a chance to write down as many of the letters as you can remember. Generally, no one remembers all of them because (cue beginning of professor's lecture) humans can reliably hold only seven (plus or minus two) things in short-term memory at a time. If this seems surprising, remember that you do not get to see the letters, you only hear them read aloud, very slowly.

The punchline is that the letters in this case can be combined into familiar chunks. Because the professor is reading so slowly, most people do not notice that the list includes three familiar American intelligence agencies (NSA, FBI, and CIA) bookended with X's. Had you noticed this, you would have easily remembered all the letters because in your mind the three letters of each agency would have been merged into individual items. This would have left you with only four items to remember (the agencies plus the bookended X's) instead of eleven, which places it within the seven-plus-or-minus-two limit.

To make this relevant to drumming, think about a time you tried to teach your friend to play a paradiddle. You rattled off a series of rights and lefts not unlike the series of letters above. When you first recited them to your friend, even if they immediately picked up on the pattern that the second half is the inverse of the first half, they almost certainly had to remember the pattern as eight individual pieces of information. If the following commas separate individual "unchunked" items, then your friend's mind was doing something like: right, left, right, right, left, right (pause, straining to remember), left, left. The individual rights and lefts had not yet been consolidated into a smaller number of chunks.

Now consider what it would feel like to have played ten thousand paradiddles in your life. At that point, you would only need to think the thought, "paradiddle," and your hands would automatically and effortlessly execute the pattern. In your memory, it has become a single item, and the thought of it has become synonymous with the action. What is most interesting about this phenomenon when applied to something like the drums is that the chunk contains both declarative and procedural memory, meaning it includes both conscious and subconscious information. At the declarative level, the entire eight-note sticking is unpacked from the drawer the instant you think the thought, "paradiddle." Furthermore, the complex motions required to execute the rudiment, which involve many synchronized movements of your fingers, wrists, and arms, are simultaneously unpacked from the same drawer.

The paradiddle is often viewed as a relatively basic rudiment, but, seen in this light, the paradiddle drawer can contain an enormous amount of information. If it includes the sticking, notation, melody, feeling, muscle memory, dynamic variations, and several orchestrations, and if all of those ways of understanding the paradiddle are well chunked and unpacked by simply recalling the "paradiddle" label, then we can say that your mental representation of that pattern is very rich. Chunking helps us see one way that it is actually neurologically accurate, if a little cliché, to say that our potential is infinite. There is no limit to the complexity of information you can chunk, nor is there a limit to how much information your long-term memory can hold.

Chunking also helps explain how master drummers are able to do incredible things with so little effort. They are limited by the seven (plus or minus two) item limit of short-term memory just like everyone else, but their Creative Directors select from a larger number of drawers that they are profoundly familiar with, each of which contains a greater quantity and complexity of information, between which they move with great fluidity. They do this with such ease that, eventually, it no longer feels that they are "making decisions" at all. What this makes clear above all else is that chunking is a mechanism that we need to leverage if we want to play more interesting things.

In Chapter 2, we established that the most important feature of any pattern or rudiment is the melody that it contains because an improviser must ultimately end up thinking in rhythmic melodies. Given what we know now about chunking, we can see that "thinking in melodies" means that *the label of a drawer must be the pattern's melody*—not the sticking, notation, counting, or something else. That way, as we allow our rhythmic stream of consciousness to flow, stringing together elements of our rhythmic vocabulary, the chunks containing the required motor coordination and sticking information get automatically unpacked and played. Now that we know that melodies must make up the label, let's figure out what type of information belongs inside the drawer.

The 5 Ways of Understanding

There are five ways of understanding melodic chunks that make them more deeply engrained and easily accessible when improvising. They include the sticking, counting, notation, feeling, and sound.

The first three of these belong to declarative memory (sticking, counting, notation), and the last two are for procedural memory (feeling, sound). The first three form your technical understanding of what you are playing. These enable you to intentionally explore alternate options, understand how different pieces fit together, and distinguish between similar but different melodic chunks. The last two ways of understanding operate at the subconscious level. Here your procedural memory must develop an automatic script for what it "feels like" to execute a pattern. "Sounds like" is your ability to recognize melodies or hear them in your mind's ear before you start consciously processing their sticking, counting, and notation.

The 5 Ways of Understanding the Paradiddle Melody

DECLARATIVE	1. Sticking	R L R R L R L L
	2. Counting	1 e & a 2 e & a
	3. Notation	
PROCEDURAL	4. Feels like	the muscle memory of playing it
	5. Sounds like	familiarity with sound of melody

The Learned-by-Ear Drummer and the Intellectualizer

Ideally, we understand each of the chunks in our drumming vocabulary equally strongly in all of the five ways described above. We can get an idea of why this is important by considering what it looks like when there are imbalances between them. The most common imbalance occurs in the *learned-by-ear drummer*. Another way to say that someone is learning by ear is to say that they are developing their procedural memory without the accompanying declarative information. They are developing physical habits that sound and feel good without knowing in any declarative, technical sense what they are doing. Sometimes this gets people surprisingly far—I have watched world-class drummers who can play things I could never dream of go on to explain them in ways that revealed that they did not technically know what they were doing—but this is only possible if you are supremely talented and manage to develop an incredible intuition along the way. Since, for the rest of us, "be more talented" is hard advice to take, developing fluency must involve understanding how things work at a technical level.

The opposite of the learned-by-ear drummer is the *intellectualizer*. These are drummers whose technical understanding of the drums is beyond their physical abilities. In psychological terms, their declarative understanding is advanced, but they have not yet spent the hundreds of hours of real practice time required to chunk the motor information that their procedural memory needs in order to execute the clever drumming ideas that they understand theoretically.

Regardless of which half of the learning process has been neglected, any imbalance makes learning and teaching difficult. Lessons can be disheartening for a learned-by-ear drummer because, even though they might be able to play many advanced things, it is difficult to methodically teach them anything new because there is no underlying framework for understanding or discussing what they are already doing. Beginning to form that framework often involves starting with basic lessons on how notation and counting work. This can be hard to swallow because these drummers might feel too advanced for such "beginner" lessons—they might even tour with really famous bands. But I find that most students immediately realize how much this is holding them back. This situation can be encouraging if the teacher emphasizes that the student has already done the hard work of practicing for thousands of hours to develop good technique, coordination, groove, and control.

On the other hand, the intellectualizer, a slightly rarer breed, is in danger of being disheartened in the opposite way. After this student has described their hopes to work on very high-level concepts during a lesson, but struggles to play several "basic" grooves when prompted, I can sometimes sense a feeling of embarrassment, as though their secret has been exposed. They are likely to say frequently that their hands are just not working today. However, as long as they are willing to begin putting in the time where it matters, they can get their hands and feet caught up with their minds in short order, and then actually start executing their great ideas.

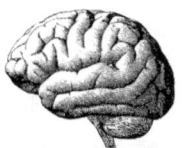

Memory

Declarative Memory

*Things you can show me
you know by telling me
(explicit facts).*

Examples:
- Capital of Alaska
- Favorite hockey player
- Paradiddle sticking

Procedural Memory

*Things you can show me
you know by doing them
(difficult to explain).*

Examples:
- Riding a bicycle
- Doing a cartwheel
- Playing a paradiddle

"Intellectualizer"

*Theoretically
understands the
technical drumming,
but can't execute.*

Limit:
Physical coordination

Balanced Understanding

Intuition
+
Understanding

"Learned by ear"

*Good intuition,
relies on feel,
minimal
understanding.*

Limit:
Rhythmic theory

I hope this is starting to make the prospect of improvising seem less mysterious and more attainable. Our job going forward is to learn to optimize the relationship between our limited short-term memory and our limitless long-term memory, and to do so in a way that balances declarative and procedural learning. This will enable us to think simple thoughts while unpacking complex chunks of drumming that are automated at the procedural level and understood at the declarative level. As the technical execution of our drumming becomes more automated, it frees up more mental energy to devote to thinking actually creative thoughts— designing the music of our playing. This brings us back to the Creative Director, whose real name is Attention, and whom we must get to know a little better if we want to feel *control* over our playing.

The Limits of The Creative Director

So far in this chapter, we have focused mainly on understanding how our minds consolidate information, which allows us to think simple thoughts while doing progressively more complex things. As drummers, we are required to do this in order to reconcile the nature of our instrument with that of our minds. The problem that our attention must constantly solve is that our instrument demands that we do many complex things at once. However, our minds are limited by the fact that we can only pay attention to one thing at a time. This attention-limit is a feature of our minds that we cannot change, and helps us understand why all the consolidation and automation we have been learning about so far is required for doing pretty much anything on the drums. Drummers who are portrayed as multi-brained machines, paying attention to several competing tasks at once, are, to the contrary, relying heavily on automated procedural memory while shifting a *single beam of attention* between tasks to monitor their execution. Understanding the limits of attention can help us understand the subtle difference between coordination and independence, which, in turn, can help us adopt more effective approaches to developing them to serve our drumming.

If you pay close attention to *attention*, you will notice two things, which are, in fact, the same thing. First, you cannot pay attention to two things at once. However, this does not mean that you cannot do two things at once. Secondly (therefore), multitasking only succeeds to the degree that one or the other task is automated. If you are listening to music while you read this book, you will notice that you cannot *actively listen* to the music (that is, follow a specific melodic line or notice a specific lyric) and *actively comprehend* what you read at the same time. You can, however, *passively hear* the music while you read, in which case it is relegated merely to background ambiance. You can also do the inverse—you can *listen to* the music while your eyes pass over the words (this, too, is automated after years of reading), but you will notice at the end of the paragraph that you have only a vague notion of what you read. If you try to read and listen actively at the same time, you will notice that you are never doing both at once, but jumping between them very quickly—a few words, a few trumpet notes, a few words, and so forth. By the end of the page, you might have gotten the gist of both, but the details and permanence of either memory will be lost. You might also notice how much more energy is required to attempt to sustain this back-and-forth, and how much less fun everything becomes.

Likewise, you can walk and have a conversation because walking is automated and requires no attention, but your conversation would pause if you needed to creep across a narrow log suspended over a stream (an activity that is not automated and demands attention). You can drive and have a conversation because driving is automated, but as soon as driving becomes challenging, the conversation stops or you lose your train of thought. You might have noticed how, as you approach a new destination in your car, you turn the music down while you look for the right house number. Turning the music down does not help you see better. It removes the music's demand on your attention, so you can direct it more reliably to the house numbers.

An imperfect but useful metaphor is that "attention is a spotlight, not a disco-ball." Earlier when I spoke about focal distance, I was talking about attention. The dimension of the spotlight we are interested in at the moment is how narrow or broad it is. When the spotlight of attention has a very narrow beam, your focal distance feels "zoomed in." When the beam of your spotlight is wide, you are taking in the whole scene. The former feels directed, while the latter feels receptive.

Visually, you can look intensely at a speck on the table, or, without moving, you can broaden your sight and see your entire field of vision. With your ears, you can narrow your attention and listen intensely only to the sound of your footsteps, or you can broaden it and hear the mix of sounds around you. You can feel the tiny tip of your thumb holding this book, or you can broaden your attention and feel your body being within the space where you are sitting. Even without the senses, we do this with our thinking. You can think about something so intensely that everything else disappears, or, as meditators try to teach, you can notice what your mind is up to. Note how the words we use change. We *listen*, or we *hear*. We *look*, or we *see*. We *feel*, or we *be*. We *think*, or we *notice*. The shift between directed and receptive attention will be important when we want to *try* something challenging, and also *hear* how it turned out.

Coordination and Independence

With the spotlight metaphor in mind, let's take a look at the difference between coordination and independence, and the two different types of automation that they rely on. Coordination happens more or less whenever you play the drums. It involves different limbs working *together*, coordinating and cooperating, to deliver an idea under a single beam of attention. When, with your attention, you supervise yourself doing something that is well coordinated, it feels like you are monitoring a single event, even if multiple limbs are involved. The automation that coordination relies on is the type of automation we learned about in the chunking section. All the movements required to play a specific pattern or melody get chunked into a single drawer and get automatically unpacked when we recall the label.

Independence, on the other hand, involves removing something from the coordinated team and assigning it a separate, repetitive task. Crucial to understanding independence is that you are removing something from the spotlight of your attention. Once automated, the limb or limbs assigned the separate job no longer place a serious demand on your attention, which allows you to focus on the coordination of the other limbs. The classic tool of independence is the *ostinato*, which is when you assign one or more limbs to repeat a pattern indefinitely while the remaining limbs play freely over top of it. To take a simple example, let's say you assign your right foot to play quarter notes on the kick drum indefinitely while you solo freely with your hands. In order to do this, playing quarter notes with your right foot needs to be sufficiently automated so that you can put it on autopilot and keep your attention focused on what your hands are doing. If it has not been sufficiently automated, and the right foot frequently messes up, then it will pull your attention away from your hands until you get it back on track. Therefore, the automation of coordination is the process of making each chunk more rich with information, while the automation of independence requires spending time repeating, and thus automating, your ostinato while you develop the coordination of your other limbs over top of it.

Although it would be nice if coordination and independence were as tidily distinct as I have made them sound, the line between them can be blurry. First of all, developing independence over an ostinato usually requires starting with *coordination* exercises that enable you to begin separating the ostinato limb from your other limbs. Even if you are quite comfortable improvising over a given ostinato, you might occasionally find yourself needing to focus on the coordination of how the ostinato interacts with a certain pattern before removing the ostinato from your attention again. Furthermore, if I am playing a repeating polyrhythm with my hands, it is possible that I have automated one hand as an ostinato in true independence style, but, over time, the melody of that polyrhythm and the coordination required to play it might become so familiar to me that it itself gets chunked as a single item, which I recall under a single beam of attention without any need for true independence at all.

Nuance aside, understanding the limits of attention is key to understanding why improvisation relies completely on automation and consolidation. To recap our precarious predicament: we can only focus on one thing at a time, and we can only hold a handful of items in mind at any given moment. Yet, our ambitious goal is to use four limbs simultaneously to explore an infinite number of options in constant succession, adhering to a strict time grid, including different ideas combined from years of study, and, what's more, we are going to make it up on the spot. Automation is necessary in order to avoid overwhelming our attention and losing control.

Attention + 5 Ways of Understanding

Let's look at attention and independence alongside the 5 Ways of Understanding (notation, counting, sticking, feel, sound). I once took a polyrhythms lab at Berklee, taught by Kenwood Dennard. At the end of the semester, he sat down at the drums, assigned different numbers to each of his limbs, and began playing the resulting four-part polyrhythm, occasionally changing one limb or another and telling us what he was doing while he did it. The memory still amazes me. To this day it remains the most impressive display of independence and coordination I have ever seen. At the time, it seemed as though he was dividing his attention, however, we know there can be no such thing. It was instead a highly demanding job for the Creative Director, who was relying on their team having a profound understanding and familiarity with overlapping rates and a deep well of independence and coordination necessary to perform them. Perhaps the Creative Director in this case is better thought of as the military drill instructor in charge not of normal recruits but of a special operations unit—the best of the best, commanded by an experienced and profoundly competent commander.

To Kenwood, not only are polyrhythms familiar to his ear, but also to his body and mind. In his class, he taught us how to understand any polyrhythm mathematically, as well as with counting and notation, and he paid particular attention to helping us become familiar with the intuitive feel and sound of each polyrhythm. In his final demonstration, Kenwood already possessed the independence required to execute these polyrhythms, and the coordination between limbs was well-established. His military drill instructor needed to constantly flit between limbs to make sure they were on track or zoom out to a monitoring position to listen to the familiar music of those overlapping rates and be on the lookout for mistakes, inconsistencies, or things starting to drift, in which case his attention would zoom in and nudge things back into alignment. If Kenwood decided to change his kick drum from quintuplets to sextuplets, his attention would momentarily narrow on the kick drum, or on the coordination between the kick drum and another limb, or on the melody that emerges from the two combined, to make sure the transition went smoothly before returning to a monitoring position. If this feels counterintuitive, it is because your attention moves between items so rapidly, constantly, and automatically that you do not notice it.

This should humanize what at first looks superhuman. Kenwood has no more attention to spare than the rest of us, and no declarative secret formula for drumming. He has the same equipment we do. Maybe he has a knack for polyrhythms, but more importantly, he has certainly spent way more time than the rest of us becoming deeply familiar with them in all the ways that matter. With only one beam of attention, be it narrow or wide, what Kenwood is helping us see is the impressive degree to which complex drumming can be automated in procedural memory.

When we see someone like Kenwood doing something so impressive yet effortless, it feels tempting to say they have a really deep *intuition* for the drums. But what does that mean? Intuition is an elusive idea, but we feel that it has something to do with creating good music. In the next couple chapters, we are going to learn several exercises that develop your drumming intuition, which is closely associated with your procedural memory. Therefore, it would be useful to first learn what intuition is, what it does for us on the drums, and how we can develop it.

Motor Intuition

As was said earlier, people usually talk about chunking in the context of expanding short-term, declarative memory (memorize 500 digits of pi type of stuff), but it is more useful for our purposes to consider how chunking facilitates mastery of a physical activity like drumming or dancing where information is stored not as declarative facts, but as unconscious muscle memory. By examining how the accumulation of experience in procedural memory gives rise to a keen intuition, we will see how it can become easy to play things that are not only correct, but which *sound good* (to you).

My wife spent her twenties as a professional dancer. At that time, we were dating and I regularly attended her performances. To state the obvious, you cannot become an excellent dancer from behind a desk. You cannot *think* your way there, at least not in the same way that you can think your way to becoming an excellent mathematician, historian, or lawyer. Dance relies on movement, which is governed by procedural memory, which, as we saw with riding a bike, is hard to quantify and teach in declarative terms. This means that dancing can only be learned by moving and imitating— by dancing—and that your ability to "dance well" is not based on the contents of your declarative memory, but on years of observing and performing movement that builds an intuition for what you consider beautiful and how to create it. Thankfully, defining "good" dance and music—which is obviously subjective and culturally dependent—is not something we need to do. Since your goal is to play music that you think is good, just inject your personal preferences whenever I use the word "good."

Your ability to create something good requires intuition. So, what is intuition, and how is it connected to declarative and procedural memory? Intuition is a feeling of rightness, and sometimes an objectively correct answer, that results from subconscious processing that is difficult or impossible to explain. Repeated engagement with relevant experiences and information is what builds the accuracy of that subconscious processing. This is why grandparents in every culture, who have accumulated the greatest amount of *life experience*, are looked to for general wisdom (intuition). Engaging with any domain, whether knowledge-based, movement-based, or a mix of the two, eventually builds intuition in this way. For example, there are many stories of mathematicians, scientists, and creatives being suddenly struck by insights, while absentmindedly riding the bus or taking a shower.[6] In these moments, it is often hard to explain the underlying logic that led to the insight because it emerged from a subconscious place. Likewise, and more relevant to our purposes, a dancer will be simply struck by a feeling that this series of movements and not that one will elicit the feeling that they hope to convey.

Therefore, reliance on intuition is something a mathematician and a dancer (and your grandmother) share, and, in all cases, intuition results from a large amount of experience engaging with relevant information. Where they differ is in the nature of the information. For mathematicians, the input is declarative, and insights presented by intuition are also declarative facts (a new equation, for example). For a dancer, the input is movement, and the output is movement. When a mathematician's intuition helps reveal a new fact, they can always reverse engineer it after the fact and discover the explanation that connects input and output. On the other hand, a master of a movement-based art can never fully explain how or why they are doing what they are doing because, to emphasize again, there is very little declarative input during the learning process. In effect, dancers have no choice but to "learn by moving." There is no blackboard equation to explain how to do a pirouette and no objective explanation as to why bending one way looks awkward and another way beautiful. Though dancing certainly involves declarative information, the dancer's intuition is fed primarily by procedural memory input—years of dancing. Amazingly, however, it responds to declarative prompts (like, *dance in a way that imitates water*). This explanation-resistant type of intuition is what I call *motor intuition*, and I like to distinguish it from regular intuition that relies more on declarative information and results in declarative facts.

Drumming is somewhere between declarative-input mathematics and procedural-input dancing. It is a dance that one does over a drum set with drumsticks, but the sounds created by the drum dance can be captured and explained approximately with stickings, notation, and counting. The fact that notation can only represent drumming *very approximately* helps us see why drumming is not math. If you give one hundred drummers the same notation, it will sound one hundred different ways. Notation cannot capture touch, feel, tone, and cannot even come close to capturing precise dynamics and placement. It cannot capture the push and pull of speeding up and slowing down, it cannot capture the intentional alignment or misalignment of notes played together, and it cannot show how a group of musicians might place their notes differently in response to one another. In short, everything that makes drumming feel human and magical cannot be declaratively represented. We need the automation of procedural memory in order to play correct music. We need intuition in order to play *good* music.

For a drummer, the building blocks of intuition come from two main sources. The first is hearing the sound of your own playing. If you remember from the attention chapter how we observed the difference between zoomed-in *listen* and zoomed out *hear*, this is a moment where you want to shift to that receptive position of hearing the music that is coming from your playing. This is only possible if what you are playing has been sufficiently automated so that you no longer need to micromanage every note along the way. Each new thing you learn starts very declarative and slowly becomes committed to procedural memory. You begin by strenuously counting, reciting stickings, and reading notation, which monopolizes your attention. You are necessarily zoomed in all the way. As what you are learning becomes more automated and demands less attention, you can shift your attention to a more receptive position and start to hear the music of your playing like an audience member.

When you do this, two things happen. First, a musical imprint (the *sounds like* way of understanding) is made at the subconscious level. This is what you ultimately pull from when you think in melodies, so this is important work. Second, you automatically start making microscopic changes to dynamics, feel, and tone—the types of changes that notation cannot capture. You might not even realize you are making these changes because, from your perspective, you are just trying to "make it groove" or "sound good."

The second source that has been developing your intuition since you were born is all the thousands of hours of music you have listened to and heard throughout your life. To a huge degree, this is what builds the foundation of your musical intuition and determines what "sounds good" in your ear. Listening to music creates expectations and preferences. Some of these are so fundamental that we no longer recognize them as expectations—common instruments, key signatures and scales, song forms, melodic and harmonic tendencies, transitions, etc. These shared foundations are why there is a good amount of agreement about something being generally good or bad. However, your specific interests, preferences, and tendencies, as well as the physiology of your body, and even your personality, affect the decisions you make as you play. Your idea of what is expected, what is powerful, or what constitutes intensity will lead you to make different decisions, even with the same vocabulary as someone else.

Furthermore, listening to music is not only passive, but can be an active way to develop your intuition. If you actively, frequently listen to a drummer with a certain style, you will find yourself absorbing certain intangible subtleties from their playing—the things of intuition. This is a powerful tool. It is also in many cases an essential one. The answer to eighty percent of the questions I have asked teachers when studying jazz has been, "Go listen to this record." This is ubiquitous to the point of cliché in jazz because traditional jazz is at the same time super improvisational and super stylistically consistent. It does not matter that you can play anything. What matters is that what you choose to play, even if innovative, is tethered to the axiomatic dynamics, melodies, and phrasing of the style, none of which can be described declaratively. Jazz is ultimately so non-declarative for drummers that the charts do not include any drum notation whatsoever. Here we see our "notation is a rough approximation" point taken to such an extreme that it would be a waste of time to write anything at all. This tension between the music being almost entirely improvised and there simultaneously being somehow a million ways to play the wrong thing is captured by the fact that the only appropriate judgment of quality is "it swings" or "it's not swinging." This is how you know you are deep in the realm of intuition, and this is when you know that actively developing your intuition is the best thing you can do for your jazz playing.

If you take into account this combination of a) deep familiarity with the music of your own drumming, and b) deeply engrained musical expectations and preferences that are mostly shared with other people, then you can see how you naturally start to automate not only correct drumming, but good music. This is the invaluable role of intuition in music, which relies heavily on *feels like* and *sounds like*— the two procedural memory ways of understanding the drums. With them so keenly developed, if you touch your instrument, not only does something correct happen, something good happens. Like a masterful dancer, if they move at all, it is beautiful.

Conclusion

Thus ends our Psychology 101 chapter. We now understand the difference between declarative and procedural memory, as well as how they rely on each other to help us think simple thoughts and play complex things. We know the 5 ways of understanding rhythms and how a balance between declarative and procedural "knowing" helps us avoid becoming learned-by-ear-drummers (lacking declarative understanding) or intellectualizers (lacking procedural automation). We learned why the limits of attention force us to rely on automation in the first place, and we saw how intuition begins to emerge and discretely improve the music of our drumming. Understanding this about our minds is not just for fun. It enables us to come up with better ways of achieving our goal. Next, we learn what types of creative exercises most effectively leverage our minds' natural tendencies and build the bridge to improvisation.

Chapter Terms

- **Procedural Memory**: Things you can show me you know by doing them. Difficult to explain. Things like juggling, buttoning a shirt, doing a cartwheel.

- **Declarative Memory**: Things you can show me you know by telling me. Explicit facts. Things like the capital of Alaska, the sticking of a paradiddle.

- **Chunking**: Your brain's ability to consolidate many pieces of information into a single "chunk." Essential for playing progressively more complex things.

- **The 5 Ways of Understanding**: Sticking, counting, notation (declarative), feeling, and sound (procedural). Leads to balanced understanding: Intuition + Understanding.

- **Attention:** Another name for the Creative Director. Can only focus on one thing at a time. Spotlight narrows to "zoom in" (analyze) and widens to "zoom out" (supervise).

- **Motor Intuition**: Your ability to recognize and create "goodness" and "beauty" in non-declarative, movement-based activities. Both the learning and the performance are at the procedural, subconscious level.

Chapter 4

Practicing Improvisation

In this chapter we are going to learn the guidelines for doing what many people consider a paradox: practicing improvisation. Surprisingly, it will never include simply sitting at your drums and playing whatever comes to mind. No skill as complex as drumming gets developed to a high level without structure. If you only experiment randomly, you will leave massive gaps in your foundation and fall into deep ruts of habit. The trick, as we will see, is to become a master at creating games with simple rules which, when mastered, propel you into improvisation with the given vocabulary. These constraint-focused games are called *creative exercises*. They build the bridge between *exercise* and *improvise*. Each creative exercise is a plank on the bridge toward fluent improvisation, laid across ropes of *continuity* that connect even the first exercises to the end goal. Creative exercises provide deep training for that non-linguistic type of memory that we now know as procedural memory.

To understand how constraints lead to control and fluency, let's turn to a natural domain for rule-based games: sports.

Drumming Like a Soccer Player

As is the case with dancing, but not with history and math, you cannot become a good soccer player by attending lectures, reading textbooks, and thinking hard. Soccer, like drumming, which happens faster than the speed of conscious deliberation, is a constant improvisation, and relies mainly on procedural memory. Therefore, an excellent soccer player needs to have already consolidated the fundamental movements of the game. What we can learn from soccer players is how to use constraints to develop controlled improvisation with a targeted subset of vocabulary. We can learn this by examining how and why soccer players balance three aspects of practice: 1) drills, 2) creative exercises, and 3) scrimmaging.

Drills and scrimmaging are pretty straightforward, and it is easy to identify the drumming equivalents. Drills involve rote repetition that trains the technical aspects of procedural memory needed to automate essential skills. For soccer, you drill things like dribbling, passing, shooting, and off-the-ball movement. For drums, you drill things by repeating rudiments, looping challenging grooves, practicing a new hand technique, or doing speed drills. Drills give you relevant raw ingredients but do not necessarily help you improvise. Playing 10,000 paradiddles does not necessarily mean you can do anything creative with them.

Scrimmaging is when you play a real game with all the real rules, but only for the sake of practicing and trying things out. The drumming equivalent of scrimmaging is when you "just play" in the practice room. You try to maintain the flow, you experiment with ideas, and you even try to make it sound good. The only difference from a real performance is that you are not on stage, the stakes are low, and your goal is simply to take everything for a test drive and see what happens. This is a "no rules" kind of practice. This sounds like it ought to be the way to practice improvising, but since creativity thrives within constraints, most drummers instead feel like they are aimlessly meandering instead of getting better at anything. Most drummers intuit that they need something between drills and scrimmaging, but are not sure what it is. They know that drills do not magically become creative, and they know that aimlessly scrimmaging does not improve anything. On one hand, we have too little freedom. On the other, too much. Enter: creative exercises.

Creative Exercises

To see how creative exercises build the bridge between *exercise* and *improvise*, we need to understand the relationship between constraints and control.

Most people's experience with trying to improvise is one of feeling completely out of control. Without constraints, trying to make sense of *all the possible options* is overwhelming. To overcome this, what we are going to do over and over again together in the coming chapters is create constraints for improvisational games. This will give us games that are simple enough to actually master, and therefore establish control. This might leave you only one small "improvisational" decision to make. Then, once control is established, we can start loosening the constraints one step at a time, reestablishing control at each step. After doing this ten or twenty times, you will find yourself improvising with a lot of variation. However, unlike before, you will understand what you are doing and feel in control. Mastering the meta-skill of strategically adjusting your own constraints to target the development of new vocabulary is one of the most important things you can learn. Let's get to know this process better with some examples.

In soccer, an example of a creative exercise is a mini-game like "Keep Away" (small space, two teams, no goals, try not to let the other team get the ball). Since the most effective way to keep the ball away from your opponents is to pass it to a teammate, we can see how the constraints are strategically designed to develop the skills of passing and moving into open space. If you are a relatively new soccer player, jumping into a 4 v 4 version of this game would feel, as with jumping into improvising, so chaotic and out of control that you would not be able to learn anything or get better. Therefore, we need to create a version of this game that is simple enough for you to master and clearly related to the more challenging version.

Let's start by giving you six other teammates in a large circle, and only one defender in the middle. The only way a single defender is going to get the ball from a team of seven is if they make an error, so this stage of the game is mostly focused on developing the specific physical patterns required to receive and pass a ball. It is mostly a technical drill, but it has continuity with our end goal in that you have one improvisational decision to make—deciding to which of your teammates you pass the ball. Once you can consistently win that game and feel in control while doing so, we can loosen the constraints one step: now you cannot pass it back to the same player who passed it to you. Then, you reestablish control. Next, your circle of teammates moves closer together, shrinking the circle, making it easier for the defender, and forcing you to react more quickly (this is sort of like increasing the tempo). Next, you and your teammates need to continually jog around in a circle while passing. Then you reverse direction. Then your team can run anywhere within the circle. Next, we add a second defender, and then three, and then four. Now you are playing 4 v 4 like we initially hoped to do.

This process might have taken weeks or months of practice, but when you take stock of your gains and assess the value, it will not seem like such a long time because you never need to do that work again. Deeply engrained procedural memory is hard to shake. That is why procedural-dependent activities come back "like riding a bike," no matter how long it has been. You now have a relatively permanent baseline of "controlled passing," which is one of the fundamental improvisational skills of the game. The value that this adds to your enjoyment of the game is enormous. Next time you play a scrimmage or game, you will be able to be more effective *and creative* on the field.

The brilliant thing about constraints is that they do the targeting for you. If constraints are set well, and they force you to use the desired vocabulary in a context that demands just the right amount of improvisation, then you develop the targeted skill more or less by accident as a result of mastering the game. If you play "Keep Away" frequently and at the right level of challenge, you cannot avoid improving your improvisational passing skills.

While all of this is happening, you are also unknowingly developing a second skill, which lives even deeper in procedural memory: the ability to solve a specific type of problem on the fly, at reflex-level speed. This is a hidden skill that improvisation depends on, and it helps us understand who, in drumming, is the "opponent" in the game.

Your Drumming Opponent

What we appear to lose when we bring these ideas into the drumming practice room is an opponent. However, one's opponent does not have to be another person. When riding a bike, your opponent is the terrain. When playing Tetris, your opponent is the randomness of the next piece. When it comes to improvisational games, the opponent is the unpredictability against which you must adapt within the constraints of the game. Mastering this moment-to-moment problem solving is what makes the activity fun. It is also what makes you good at the activity, which in turn makes it more fun, and so forth.

Framed this way, we can identify our drumming opponent. Assuming we are playing alone, our opponent comes not from other unpredictable people, but from the very fact that you are attempting to form new combinations in real time faster than your conscious mind can follow. As you approach the end of this or that combination, you might get spit out on an unexpected count that you do not usually accent. Or maybe the pattern does not get you all the way back to Beat 1 and you suddenly need to fill the remaining space of the measure. To improvise is to encounter a continuous stream of small problems that require nearly-automatic responses. This is why, after decades of improvisation, it remains full of surprises. You must be constantly on your toes, focused and present, to react to unforeseen circumstances which continue to appear even when your playing is centered on familiar vocabulary.

To frame our present state, we now have two problems wrapped up together that are preventing us from improvising. As discussed earlier, we have the problem of rhythmic vocabulary, and now we have the problem of not being able to adapt to the problems that constantly arise when you combine ideas on the fly. The first is a melodic problem, the second is a coordination problem. Expanding your rhythmic vocabulary often means that your coordination needs to improve in order to play the new melodies. To complete the feedback loop, improving your coordination enables you to play a wider array of melodies in more varied ways. You can see both of these problems at play in the following example.

I often ask new students to "play the drums without playing a groove," or to "play an infinite drum fill," so that I can get an idea of their improvising comfort zone. To most drummers, this exercise feels like attempting to juggle for the first time. It is obvious how to begin (throw the balls into the air) but impossible to keep going. Before beginning, students usually give me a "here goes nothing" type of shrug, and then proceed to play something familiar. After a few seconds, most stumble or run out of gas, and we can now see why. If the student had a broad rhythmic vocabulary, they would not necessarily be limited by a lack of coordination because they could play interesting and unique melodies orchestrated in simple ways. However, since we know that rhythmic vocabulary is often lacking, what more frequently happens is a second type of stumble. In the heat of attempting to combine patterns, most get stumped by some problem that appears that they did not anticipate and could not react to quickly enough—they ended on a left hand when they were expecting to end on a right; an unfamiliar melody emerged from their playing and confused their sense of time; or trying to throw in some bass drums made the whole thing collapse. Even if they know many patterns, they are not yet able to quickly find connecting pieces to bridge the awkward gaps that constantly appear. Like we defined above, these awkward gaps, surprising melodies, and inversions of your stickings are your "opponents" when you scrimmage your drums, and you successfully play the game when you can adapt to them quickly enough not to interrupt the flow of time. Thus our creative exercises will help us build this reflex-speed problem-solving vocabulary.

Conclusion

We now have a deep understanding of the challenges of improvisation and the types of training that help us surmount them. We know that rhythmic vocabulary is the root of all creative drumming, but we still need concrete methods for expanding it. We know that carefully designed creative exercises give us games that are simple enough to master, which enable us to maintain control as we add variation, but we do not yet have specific examples. In the next chapter, we move from theory to practice by learning three specific strategies that simultaneously develop our rhythmic vocabulary, our coordination, and our ability to adapt to problems in real time. As we now know, the bridge between *exercise* and *improvise* does not build itself, and the edge of that gap is where many drummers find themselves stuck—with good technique, speed, and coordination, but without a way of methodically practicing and developing controlled improvisation.

Chapter Terms

- **Creative Exercise:** A "game" where you improvise within set rules. Allows you to maintain control while progressively adding variation. Trains procedural memory.

- **Constraints:** The rules you set for your creative exercises. These allow you to target specific patterns and skills that you want to improvise with.

- **Control:** Understanding what you play as you play it. The opposite of guessing.

- **Your Opponent:** Unexpected problems that constantly occur when combining drumming ideas in real time.

Chapter 5

Melodic Strategies

As described in Chapter 2, the most important lightbulb moment of my teaching career was realizing how few of my students could come up with interesting melodies from scratch. As we now know, what they were missing was rhythmic vocabulary. To address this, my students needed more than just a long list of individual melodies to memorize. Improvisation is an unfolding process, tethered to the passing of time, so what they needed were strategies that helped them play *continuous* melodies—melodies that can go on for minutes that the student understands and can manipulate along the way. Improvisation depends on this underlying skill. This is where *melodic strategies* come in.

Melodic strategies are ways of coming up with melodies on the drums. They come in many forms, and are largely responsible for making a non-improviser into an improviser. To develop the three strategies of this chapter, we will use what we learned in the previous chapter and make creative exercises that simplify the rules of an improvisational game to the point where you can master it. Then we will systematically loosen the constraints and maintain control along the way.

Adding in the psychology terms from Chapter 3, melodic strategies help us think about continuous melodies in the concrete terms of declarative memory, which we can use to train and guide our subconsciously-driven procedural memory. This then gives us the balance between declarative and procedural understanding that builds both intuition and control. Put in our metaphorical terms from Chapter 2, the team's (your limbs) entire job is to deliver rhythmic melodies to the drums. If the Creative Director does not have a declarative way of thinking about unfolding melodies, and can only ambiguously request, "Make something. Anything!" then the team will be left stabbing in the dark, creating the same habitual product over and over again

Crucially (and fortunately), melodic strategies are *skills* that anyone can learn. The three strategies I am going to explain in this chapter are ones that I have found to be particularly high-leverage. Each strategy is useful in different contexts because each gives rise to a musically unique way of drumming. Furthermore, the strategies feel uniquely different when you do them, which reminds us that the feeling of improvisation is not the same experience from moment to moment. The three strategies we will learn in this chapter are representative of three broader approaches that we will get to know along the way: 1) the Building Blocks Approach, 2) the Unfolding Melody Approach, and 3) the Drop & Go Approach. Let's start by returning to our beloved paradiddle.

#1: The Building Blocks Approach

With the Building Blocks Approach, we take multiple patterns of the same length and learn to rearrange them on the fly, placing them one after the next in an unbroken chain. Since each block contains a different melody, rearranging them on the fly results in a constant flow of melodic playing that you can control. This approach is a great first foray into improvisation, and gives us a particularly clear chance to see how chunking works in action.

Let's assume that you can already play a paradiddle (RLRR LRLL). A paradiddle drawer exists, chunked away in memory. It contains the sticking and the motor information to execute it, but you have not yet noticed a melody embedded in the paradiddle, or the counting and notation of that melody. Currently, the label of the drawer is not the pattern's melody, but instead its sticking. This means that when you think to play a paradiddle, you think "RLRR LRLL" and do not hear much of a melody happening. Since we are not going to ultimately "think in stickings," we first want to discover the rudiment's melodic content and start identifying it by that as much as possible.

To begin, I ask you to play the right hand loudly and the left hand softly (ghost notes) so we can hear the "right hand melody." I call this way of playing *right hand lead*, and it gives us one way of extracting a melody from a rudiment. We repeat this until it is effortless. I ask you to sing the melody of the right hand while you play, then sing it without playing, so that what it *sounds like* starts to become familiar.

Then we write down the *notation* and *counting* of the melody and begin associating it with the *feel* and *sound* of the *sticking* (all five ways of understanding). After plenty of repetition, when you see the *notation* of the melody, you automatically and effortlessly play the paradiddle *right hand lead*. You are still just playing a paradiddle, but you are using the melody embedded in the rudiment to transcend "thinking in stickings" and start "thinking in melodies."

Finding the "Right Hand Melody" of the Paradiddle

The paradiddle sticking: **R L R R   L R L L**

The "right hand melody:"

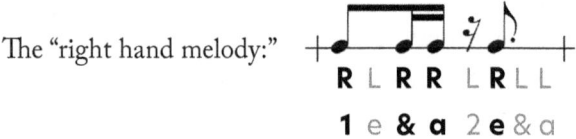

R L R R   L R L L
1 e & a   2 e & a

Next, I give you three other permutations of the paradiddle and ask you to learn them in the same way (a permutation is when you scoot the pattern over and start it in a different place). Each permutation contains its own unique melody. We follow the same process until the sight of the notation for each of the four permutations automatically triggers your effortless performance of it. You have now thoroughly chunked four individual melodic blocks, and can start to practice rearranging them. To do this, you take the numbers

1, 2, 3, and 4, and randomize them on paper. When you see 1, you play the melody from the first paradiddle. When you see 2, you play the second, and so forth. First example: 1, 2, 3, 4. Next: 3, 2, 4, 1. Next: 2, 2, 1, 3, etc. In each of these examples, you are playing 32 notes, but you are only thinking about four items (chunks). Crucially, each chunk contains melodic information, which is what we were prioritizing during the learning process.

"The 4 Paradiddles" and Their Right Hand Melodies

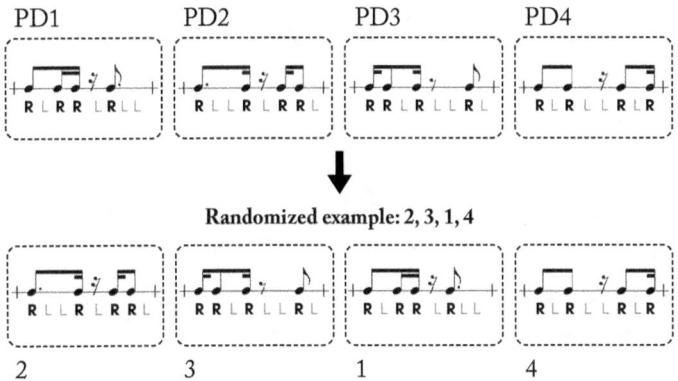

After several written examples like those above, I ask you to start randomizing the numbers in your head without stopping. First, we sing instead of play, to make sure we are thinking in melodies, then we do it on the drums. The chunks are very familiar at this point, but you begin at a slow tempo because the skill of mentally rearranging them is new and unpracticed. You visualize the number 1, then 3, then 2, then

2, 3, 1, 4, etc. If you did this every day for a while, eventually you would even stop thinking of the numbers—you would be thinking melodically! To test you, I would sing a melody that uses these patterns, but I would not specify which ones were being used. You would play it back *also without thinking about which patterns were required* (because you are thinking melodically). However, if I asked you to tell me which numbers the melody corresponded to, you would be able to. Now you are playing from *feels like* and *sounds like*, but, crucially, you also have the underlying *counting, notation,* and *sticking* knowledge, which will now allow you to make intentional changes.

At this point, you are successfully making one small improvisational decision: *which block comes next?* This tightly constrained creative exercise has continuity with our end goal because you are thinking in melodies, and developing the internal skill of rearranging patterns on the fly, which is one of the essential skills of improvisation. The rules are still so tightly constrained that this will feel more like an exercise than improvisation, but that is OK. Creative exercises usually begin more on the exercise side, and slowly become more creative. For example, what happens next with the Building Blocks Approach is that you reach a certain tipping point, at which, having done so much systematic, controlled rearranging, you develop enough coordination, enough familiarity with the melodies, and enough ease in playing them, that you start to be able to explore all sorts of *adjacent* melodies that were never on your pre-determined list. And you do it on the fly. Many of these will be just a note or two different from the 4 Paradiddles, but they each contain a new melody (for example, RRLR LRLL).

What you end up doing then, quite naturally, is playing melodies "in the style of" the 4 Paradiddles. You frequently return to the safe base of the original patterns, but you have enough control and free attention to continually, and even systematically, try adjacent ideas. As you consciously (declaratively) notice the sticking and melody of a new pattern, it forms its own drawer very quickly because it is so similar to the original patterns. Subconsciously (procedural memory), the feeling of playing it and the sound of the melody get stored as well. Now you are really exploring patterns on the fly, but you are able to keep one foot in the comfort zone that you developed with the 4 Paradiddles and return there from moment to moment as needed. In the beginning, you spend most of your time in the comfort zone and only venture out for one or two patterns at a time. Eventually, you develop enough control to stay with new patterns for longer before needing to return. At this point, you will start to feel like you are really surfing the wave of improvisation.

What starts to happen when you are exploring in a tightly controlled space like this is that the various drawers of individual patterns become very tightly connected. You begin to create a drawer of drawers. Once you play this game for long enough, it becomes so easy for you to move between all these adjacent patterns that it feels like you, as the Creative Director, simply flip a switch to turn on the whole

"4-Paradiddles-Style Right-Hand-Lead Flow" machine. You open the drawer of drawers and out flows effortless melodic improvisation within the constraints. Like I said above, you can see how this drawer contains both infinite possibilities as well as musical limitations. Starting to orchestrate, add dynamics, add space, change tempo, and include the kick drum will exponentially increase the creative potential, but, on the other hand, the constraints of the game necessarily keep your playing within certain musical boundaries.

This 4 Paradiddles example is only one melodic strategy within the broader Building Blocks Approach. The approach can be applied to all sorts of different styles of playing by choosing different building blocks. For example, I often use the Building Blocks Approach to teach improvisational freedom with a certain type of fast linear groove that I call a *flow groove*. Instead of using the 4 Paradiddles, I use what I call the 16 Invisible Rhythms, which are 16 high-leverage patterns (melodies) that are creatively common and useful. If you learn to move between even a handful of them, you quickly find yourself improvising the types of grooves that most people associate with very advanced drumming.

Given that there are thousands of possible patterns you could do this with, the Good Teacher helps you determine which patterns will be high leverage for the type of vocabulary you want to build. If you use the Building Blocks Approach to develop triplet fill vocabulary, for example, you will need a set of triplet patterns that work well enough to get you to the tipping point.

What I love about the Building Blocks Approach is that for each set of blocks, the patterns themselves are a means to an end. You use them to develop a comfort zone, and then become an expert at exploring adjacent vocabulary to the extent that eventually you no longer think much about the original patterns. I find this comforting as a teacher because it means that the stakes are low. We just need a set of patterns that are good enough.

You can see how different this is to studying a long, exhaustive list of possible patterns. This would fail to get us to the tipping point that leads to real improvisation. Remember, we can only hold a handful of things in working memory at a time. Working with too many options at once prevents us from consolidating any of them. You can remember and rearrange four blocks on the fly, but you cannot do that with 30. Even with the 16 Invisible Rhythms, we never work with all of them at once, but in smaller groups. Instead of filling a small number of drawers with deep understanding so that we can explore adjacent melodies, studying all the patterns ever would be like having hundreds of slips of paper scattered around the floor that we keep picking up, looking at, and dropping again. We would never commit them to declarative or procedural memory. It is the act of repeated processing that facilitates deep familiarity, automation of execution, and allows you to ultimately transcend the patterns you started with and improvise in the style that was captured by them. As you explore adjacent options, you might find that you even replace the "core" patterns with new ones that you think sound better. This is how dozens of drummers start studying the same material and end up sounding completely different.

Melodies Are Transferable (And This Is a Big Deal)

Now that we understand what it means to think melodically, we can reveal the enormous benefit of doing so: melodies are transferable. Let's go back to the creative exercise with the 4 Paradiddles where you are rearranging the numbers 1-4 in your head and playing the resulting melodies in an unbroken chain. Now, instead of playing those melodies with your right hand, you play them on your kick drum and remove the left-hand completely. The right hand melody has become a kick drum melody. Since you are thinking melodically, you can keep rearranging the four chunks in your head the same as you just were, but deliver the melody to your foot instead of your hand. Now add eighth notes on the hihat and a backbeat on Beats 2 and 4. Now you are using the Building Blocks Approach, with the same steps, all the way up to the tipping point where you start really improvising, but you are playing the melodies on your kick drum underneath a groove.

Then you could radically change the setting again, still using the same melodies and approach, and you could play a samba foot pattern and play all of the 4-Paradiddle melodies as flams with your hands. If you are a metal-head, you could play those melodies on a China cymbal while you play constant 16th notes on the double kick and a halftime backbeat.

Paradiddle Melodies Played On
the Kick Under a Groove

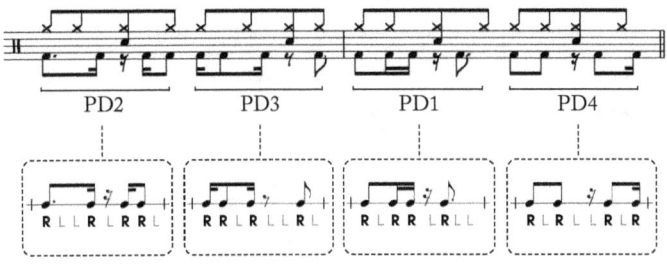

Rhythmic melodies transfer in a way that stickings do not. I am not a fan of using the word, "hack," but melodic strategies are as close to a drumming hack as we are going to get. This is why, when people ask me how I learned sets of complicated *progressive metal* music (Periphery, Animals as Leaders, Steve Vai) when asked to sub with only a few days' notice, I explain that it was thanks to all the *big band jazz* I played as a teenager, where I spent hundreds of hours reading notation and internalizing rhythmic melodies. Even between these seemingly disparate genres of music, the rhythmic melodies are the same. They are *always* the same. Mastering rhythmic vocabulary makes you more than just creative—it makes you versatile because all types of music rely on the same underlying rhythmic melodies.

The Glue

In addition to seeing how chunking works in action, the Building Blocks Approach shows us another essential subconscious tool that is being developed during a creative exercise: *the glue*. In the 4 Paradiddles example, the tipping point was the point where you were so in control of rearranging the pre-determined patterns that you could try to plug in a new but similar pattern on the fly. As soon as you begin doing this, you find yourself encountering small problems. For example, a pattern might spit you out on a weird count or on the wrong hand, or it might cause you to play too many notes with one hand in a row. The glue consists of all the little bits of drumming that fill spaces and help you adapt to that steady stream of surprises inherent to improvisation.

The glue can apply itself technically, like when you need to add a note or two in order to fit patterns together, but also physically, like when the physical awkwardness of trying to do something gets resolved in the moment successfully. It is essential to understand that the glue cannot be developed through declarative, knowledge-based technical exercises. There is simply no way to study all the little pieces of drumming you might need to use to get from one pattern to any of a hundred other patterns, and these patterns will *always* be passing too quickly for you to "choose" the right bit of glue consciously from declarative memory.

The glue is the other thing we develop in creative exercises like "Keep Away" and the Building Blocks Approach. When you methodically engage with the right amount of unpredictability, like you do in a well-designed creative exercise, you simultaneously develop (consciously) your control rearranging the patterns and (subconsciously) *the glue*. Recall the "here goes nothing" shrug that many students gave before attempting to play a never-ending drum fill. Without constraints that simplify the game, improvising presented too many problems too quickly for their gluing systems to handle.

Incidentally, the relationship we have described between constraints and control is also what makes a game fun, and what makes mastery rewarding. When you improvise, it maintains a certain unpredictability even to you, the player. Pleasant surprises and small, manageable obstacles are part of the activity itself. The pleasure increases as you become more advanced because you create with greater complexity and encounter a wider array of new challenges, which you are at the same time more prepared to respond to.

The Building Blocks Approach showed us chunking in action—we reduced four 8-note patterns (32 notes) into four richly understood, easily recalled items. We facilitated this by learning the 4 Paradiddles in a way that balanced declarative and procedural memory, and we prioritized the melody, showing us what it means to "think melodically." We undertook our first creative exercise of rearranging those four blocks on the fly. This had continuity with our goal, and got us to the tipping point where rearranging was easy enough that we could start exploring adjacent patterns on the fly. We saw how tight constraints gave us an entry point where the rules were simple enough to master, and we saw that the process of slowly loosening those constraints was the process of building our options and glue while maintaining control. We also showed how the melody-making that we learn in one context can transfer to other contexts, making us generally more creative and versatile, which underscores the value of rhythmic vocabulary and, therefore, melodic strategies. All of this will remain true as we explore our second approach.

#2: The Unfolding Melody Approach

Like in the first example, the Unfolding Melody Approach involves limiting ourselves to certain rules that, when followed, create a continuous melody. The difference is that with the Building Blocks Approach, the melodies are contained *within the blocks*; whereas, with the Unfolding Melody Approach, the melody emerges as a result of us simply following the rules. I use several melodic strategies within this approach, but my favorite is the *Down-Up Method*. Here's how it works.

As you can see below, the eighth note counts are the "downs" (downbeats). That's 1 & 2 & 3 & 4 &. The 'e's and 'a's are the "ups" (upbeats). You can think of the downbeats and upbeats as two parallel tracks running side-by-side.

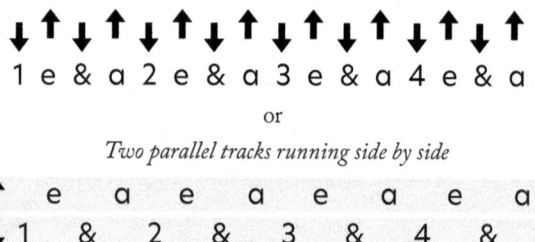

or

Two parallel tracks running side by side

Like we did in the Building Blocks Approach, let's play right hand lead, meaning your right hand plays the melody on a rack tom and your left hand plays ghost notes on the snare drum. The goal is to play consecutive 16th notes and have your right hand jump between the downbeat track and the upbeat track at will. Your left hand will fill in the ghost notes along the way. You have to play at least two downs or ups in a row before switching. Below is an example of a one-measure melody. Notice how it starts with downbeats, then jumps to the upbeat on the 'a' of Beat 2, stays there for three upbeats, then jumps back to downbeats on Beat 4.

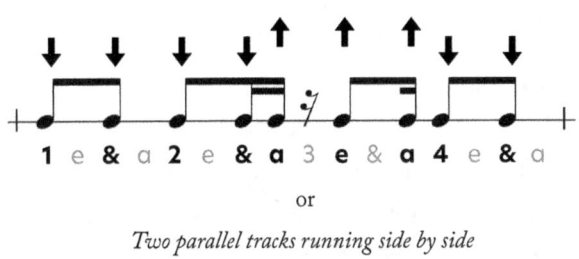

or

Two parallel tracks running side by side

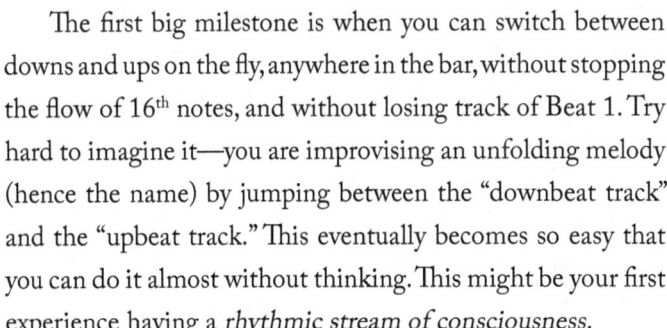

The first big milestone is when you can switch between downs and ups on the fly, anywhere in the bar, without stopping the flow of 16th notes, and without losing track of Beat 1. Try hard to imagine it—you are improvising an unfolding melody (hence the name) by jumping between the "downbeat track" and the "upbeat track." This eventually becomes so easy that you can do it almost without thinking. This might be your first experience having a *rhythmic stream of consciousness.*

Like usual with the first, most tightly-constrained creative exercise, it sounds pretty boring. The constraints are too tight to have any variety, but they had to be that tight in order to give us an entry point where we could establish control and understanding. From this improvisational but monotonous milestone, a staggering amount of variety can be developed.

Let's imagine we are able to do the Down-Up Method, as it is described above, relatively effortlessly. Now let's loosen the constraints one step at a time and multiply our creative options. First, let's allow our right hand to orchestrate freely around the drums (manageable coordination problems occur, and control is reestablished). Then we orchestrate it on the cymbals too, adding a kick drum whenever we play the cymbal (balance issues occur when playing the kick, and physical control is reestablished). Then we look at each left hand ghost note as a potential accent. As you start to accent one here and there, some of them confuse your ear because it changes the melody significantly (confusing melodies emerge, and familiarity and control are reestablished). Then we start converting right hand accents into ghost notes. This allows us to add space without needing to stop the down-up scroll that is rolling through our mind. All of these steps give us new orchestration options while leaving the underlying down-up melody untouched.

Let's move on to bigger changes. You can now practice the Down-Up Method *left-hand-lead*, and repeat all of the steps from before. Then you can practice moving between right-hand and left-hand lead. You replace melody notes with kick drums, making our flow momentarily kick-drum-lead. Conversely, you replace the ghost notes with kick drums, giving us a bombastic assault of hand accents and kicks. Each of these ideas is first explored as the sole variation, but slowly they are mixed together. Some of them require going back to exercises to build up new coordination or melodic familiarity. However, since it is all based on the Down-Up Method, which you have already mastered, each variation feels like a small and attainable step. Eventually, each evolution of the initial creative exercise becomes easy to do. When you step back and survey your creative options, you have enormous variety in the ways you can deliver this unfolding melody to the drum set. You can orchestrate one or both hands, add space, add cymbals, add kick drum in various ways, and switch to left hand lead, not to mention adjusting the dynamics or stopping and starting the flow. As you jump between these ideas and combine them, the underlying melodic stream of consciousness rolls right along.

If we want to think again about the magic of music, this is an important moment, not so much for you as for your audience. There are three levels of magic. The first: no magic. You follow simple rules without much room for variation and you are fully conscious of every note you are playing. Likewise, your audience can easily recognize the rules of the game, and they feel like they are watching a drill.

The second level is what we have just achieved: magic for the audience. You just mastered so many creative exercises based on the Down-Up Method, and you can move between them so fluidly, that your audience has no chance of figuring out what you are thinking. You are officially thinking simple thoughts and playing complex things. The variation seems infinite, yet it feels musically focused because it is all based on a single underlying melodic strategy.

The third level is what we strive for and the reason we do all this work in the first place: magic for you, too. As we will describe in greater detail in the next chapter, you will slowly arrive at a point where the rhythmic stream of conscious flows so freely, you move between orchestration ideas so swiftly, and you explore adjacent vocabulary so constantly, that you find yourself frequently unable to account for where new ideas are coming from. Not only correct, not only good, but even *novel* drumming seems to be *happening to you.*

Down-Up, Up, and Away

Depending on where you are in your drumming journey, the little taste of magic described above is either exciting or intimidating. You might be thinking, "Are there really fifty sets of creative exercises like the one we just described?" Absolutely, and way more. However, there is a snowball effect that saves you from needing to start from scratch every time. For example, dozens of creative exercises branch off of the original Down-Up Method. With the original method mastered, you have already done half the work for every subsequent version. Generalizability was one of the tenets of our philosophy that we talked about in Chapter 1. This is where the Down-Up Method shows its potential. It is useful in almost any drumming context, and can be adapted into hundreds of exercises for all levels of drumming.

Because the Down-Up Method is a way of thinking of melodies that is not attached to any specific stickings, we can leverage it further by exchanging the current stickings for different ones. Since we have already mastered the underlying melodic strategy, this allows us to multiply our vocabulary over and over again with every new set of stickings. One of my students' favorite variations is based on the sticking, RLLK, and it uses an adaptation of the Down-Up Method that I call the "4-2 Down-Up." If your '4' pattern is RLLK, and your '2' pattern is RL, you can rearrange the 4's and 2's on the fly to create an unfolding melody. The resulting melody that you play with your right hand will be a Down-Up Melody. Then, like we did with the 4 Paradiddles and the original Down-Up Method, we can chunk the stickings and recall them by simply thinking of the numbers 4 and 2, or, better yet, of the arrow notation shown below. Just like that, the Down-Up Method enables us to quickly start improvising an unfolding melody with patterns that are totally new to us. The framework provided by the Down-Up Method helps us to do this systematically, which helps us establish control. In the example in the next image, we keep the same Down-Up Melody that we used in the previous example, but now it is applied to the 8th note grid, meaning the downbeats are the counts $(1, 2, 3, 4)$ and the upbeats are the &'s.

The Same Down-Up Melody with 4's and 2's

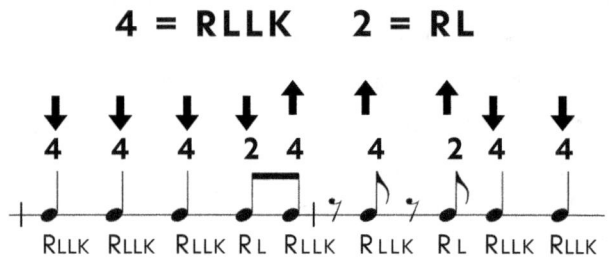

This is just one example of a pair of stickings, but you can substitute other groups of 4 and 2 for these. You could make the '4' a paradiddle (RLRR or LRLL) and make the '2' into the sticking RL or LR, and you would have another way of making paradiddles creatively useful. You can do the same process with groups of 6 and 3 as well as groups of 8 and 4.

To drill the point home, a single melodic strategy can have massive potential, and the Down-Up Method is merely one method that fits within the Unfolding Melodies Approach. Other variations of the Down-Up Method include the Swung Down-Up, the 3-Over-2 Down-Up, the 6-3 Down-Up, and more. Within each of these variations, there exist many possible sticking combinations. Other versions of the Unfolding Melody Approach do not rely on downs and ups at all, but take a repeating group of 3, 5, or 6 as their base. I chose the Down-Up Method for demonstration because the rules are relatively easy to explain in text and it continues to prove an impressively useful tool for all levels of drumming—I summon the Down-Up Method when I drum just as frequently as my beginner students do. Now let's turn to a third, very different, melodic strategy that, once learned, will always be close at hand.

#3: The Drop & Go Approach

With the Drop & Go Approach, we define a small set of melodic fragments and practice dropping them into the flow one at a time at all the possible locations. The most common way to use this approach is in a groove context, where your hands maintain the hihat and backbeat, and you systematically move the fragments through the grid on the kick drum. The improvisational goal is to be able to sprinkle in any fragment on any count on the fly. These constraints give you another simple melody-making game that you can master. Once you start sprinkling melodic fragments at will, they get combined in the ear of the listener to form longer and more varied melodies, which disguises the simple game you are really playing.

Since the vast majority of a drummer's time is spent playing grooves where the kick drum plays all the melodic content, this is a high-leverage area for making your drumming more varied and creative. In fact, no matter what type of groove you are hoping to improvise with, the first step can almost always be to expand your kick drum rhythmic vocabulary with the Drop & Go Approach. Where the Down-Up Method was an example of generalizability in solo and fill contexts, the Drop & Go Approach is the same for a groove context, making improvisation in all types of grooves easier in general.

Let's get into a standard 8th note groove and see how this works. Your right hand is playing 8th notes on the hihat. Your left hand is playing backbeats on Beat 2 and 4. This is the classic rock beat. In the following image, the 16th note grid is shown below the notation. We want to be able to drop our melodic fragments on any of these counts. Below the notation, you can see the fragments that we ultimately want to be able to sprinkle in at will. Fragments A, B, and C do not include doubles (two 16th notes in a row). Since doubles can be challenging to play, they are grouped together as fragments D, E, and F.

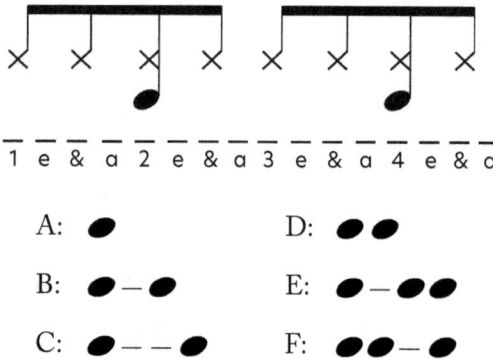

The process of running the drills is pretty self-explanatory. Choose one fragment at a time and move it through the grid. Many teachers use some version of a "grid system" like this with their students, which is a good sign that it is a useful strategy. However, I generally see it used only as an independence and coordination drill as opposed to a creative strategy. The problem, which is very familiar to us now, is that technical drills do not magically turn into improvisational fluency. A series of creative exercises is needed to build the bridge from *exercise* and *improvise*.

For the Drop & Go Approach, an example of an early creative exercise involves choosing a single melodic fragment and then limiting yourself to a single improvisational decision: where you place it. Let's say you drilled melodic fragment 'B' to the point where you feel confident placing it on any count that you choose. A great additional drill would be for me to show you randomized flash cards that tell you where to place it in the bar, one after the next, and for you to drop the fragment accordingly without ever stopping the time. Next, we cross the tipping point into improvisation and move the flashcards into your head. You decide where you drop the fragment. At first, you might place only one 'B' per measure, to get used to choosing on the fly. Then you place two within a measure. As you explore, you listen to the melodies that emerge, noticing that when the two fragments are close together, they come across as one larger melody. Then, you try three 'B' fragments in one measure, and you find something like this groove:

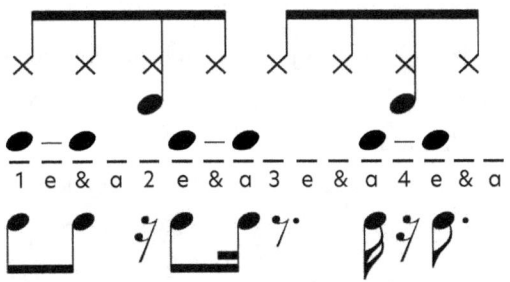

If you played this groove, no one would ever guess that you were thinking about sprinkling a single melodic fragment throughout the bar because, to the listener, the entire melody comes across as one idea. This is another example of thinking simple thoughts while playing complex things. We are starting to create a useful asymmetry between you and the listener. You know the simple rules of the game you are playing, but they receive something that seems much more complex and ever-changing.

Once this creative exercise is under control, we can loosen the constraints by adding a second fragment (let's say 'B' and 'C'). The goal then is to freely sprinkle in both 'B' and 'C' on the fly. That would probably push you past the edge of your control, so you could narrow the constraints by saying you must play 'B' first and 'C' second, and each one can only be played once per measure. We constantly monitor our out-of-control-meter to keep it below the red zone.

Eventually, systematically, through the process of strategically adjusting the constraints, we could work up to the point where you allow yourself all of the fragments. Now the game is to drop any fragment anywhere in the bar on the fly. Like we saw with jumping straight into 4 v 4 Keep Away, if we had tried to jump straight to this step after our drills, we would have felt completely overwhelmed. It seems paradoxical, but when we jump directly into the deep end of overwhelming complexity, we tend to develop a small set of familiar patterns and get stuck playing them. We have to inch toward complexity, step by step, because the mental skills required to cope with it—in this case, choosing fragments and placements in real time—is a skill in itself that we need to build up alongside our technical abilities.

Now that we know the full arc of this strategy, moving from drills to creative exercises to fluency, we can bring greater continuity to even the earliest steps. The drilling stage is straightforward—choose a fragment and move it along the grid. However, the danger with drills that require repetition is that it is tempting to do them *mindlessly*. With certain aspects of drumming, like speed and technique, practicing for an hour while you watch TV can be justified. However, when you are working to develop your melody-making, you never want to practice mindlessly. It is the act of paying attention, of receptively hearing your playing, that allows these melodic phrases to seep into your subconscious and form musical imprints at the level of procedural memory (*sounds like, feels like*). The final experience of fluent improvisation with the Drop & Go Approach is not one where you constantly select a fragment, a count, and execute one drill after another. It is one where you set your rhythmic stream of consciousness to "Drop & Go" mode," and begin letting them flow out. When needed, you more intentionally place certain fragments in certain places, but then you zoom back out and allow the melodic stream of consciousness to take charge again.

The difference is important. We do not want improvisation to feel like just another exercise (no magic), and "thinking melodically" should not ultimately feel like doing an exercise at all. However, thinking melodically does not magically happen all of a sudden. As *continuity* keeps reminding us, even the mental tools need to be developed in stages along the way. If you have ever asked yourself, "When am I ready to move on to the next exercise?" the answer with melodic strategies is: once you can hear the music of your playing.

Improving What You Hear in Your Head

Students often say they just want to be able to play what they hear in their heads. This is all well and good, but I would propose that this is mostly an illusion. Without an underlying framework with which to think about rhythms, like the ones we are building in this book, what we tend to hear in our heads is a vague echo of good drumming that we have encountered in songs and videos. If you do not have structured ways of creating melodies on the drum set, then you are almost certainly not hearing those melodies in your head. If some polyrhythm is foreign to your hands, or if dotted eighth notes are confusing, then they are almost certainly foreign and confusing to your mind's ear. What you find as you develop melodic strategies and deepen your 5 Ways of Understanding is that "what you hear in your head" begins to change. Those vague echoes begin to be replaced by the melodies and orchestrations that you can actually play, thanks to the balanced, underlying framework of understanding you are building in your practice.

If you imagine what your favorite drummer hears in their head when they think about the drums, you almost certainly imagine perfect synchrony between a) what they can play, b) what they can sing, and c) what they hear in their head. This state is not achieved by them having raised the level of their playing until it meets a vision that always existed in their head. It is all profoundly intertwined. As you do creative exercises and learn melodic strategies with all the 5 Ways of Understanding; as you expand your rhythmic vocabulary along with your coordination and independence; as your rhythmic stream of consciousness flows with more variety; as you learn to think melodically with control; and as you automate a wide variety of stickings along the way, you begin to carry around a more high-resolution representation of drumming in your mind. Thinking about playing the drums starts to feel very similar to actually playing the drums. As this alignment develops, you find that you can actually work out drumming ideas in your head, and that you can even make progress developing new ideas to a certain degree without even touching the kit. Notice and nurture this process because it represents your growing mastery of the instrument. If you imagine any master of any activity, you can assume that they carry around that activity in their mind in near-perfect detail.

Conclusion

In this chapter, all of our theory finally showed us, in concrete terms, what practicing improvisation looks like on the drums. Within three separate approaches, we learned three melodic strategies, and a number of variations of those strategies, each of which helped us develop improvisational freedom with progressively more vocabulary. We can now see how the meta-skill of setting strategic constraints is key to slowly building a large amount of improvisational vocabulary. Since the approaches covered in this chapter are very generalizable, you will quickly start to master not only specific strategies, but the meta-skill of strategically adjusting constraints in general, which will make you a more self-sufficient learner. All that we are still missing is a way of conceptualizing, organizing, and mixing all of this quickly-growing vocabulary together. To do this, we need a model for integrating *all* of our drumming vocabulary.

Chapter Terms

- **Melodic Strategies:** Ways of coming up with rhythmic melodies on the drums that you can understand and control. Developed through creative exercises.

- **The Building Blocks Approach:** A type of melodic strategy where you rearrange multiple patterns of the same length on the fly. A great first foray into improvisation.

- **The Glue:** The little bits of drumming that solve the stream of problems that occur when rearranging patterns on the fly.

- **The Unfolding Melody Approach:** A type of melodic strategy where following the rules produces an unfolding rhythmic melody we can manipulate on the fly.

- **The Down-Up Method:** A melodic strategy where you create unfolding melodies by jumping back and forth between downbeats and upbeats. An example of the Unfolding Melody Approach.

- **The Drop & Go Approach:** A type of melodic strategy where you drop melodic fragments into the flow of time at will. Most useful in a groove context.

Chapter 6

Integration

In the last two chapters, we learned how to develop a lot of improvisational vocabulary. In this chapter, we are going to learn how to conceptualize and integrate *all* of that vocabulary together. If our vocabulary is not well-integrated, we risk developing several isolated pockets of improvisational vocabulary we cannot combine. Therefore, for our purposes, *integration* means two things. First, it means developing ways of moving between different parts of your vocabulary seamlessly. Second, it means learning something new in a way that makes it permanent, which requires incorporating it into your existing vocabulary. To do this, we will leverage the way that your mind naturally "organizes" itself by forming webs of relevance. A drumming version of this model is shown in the following image. We will learn that clusters on this web are called *subsets*. Subsets are the linchpin of integration. They facilitate the consolidation of existing material, the retention of new material, and provide one of the simplest and most valuable creative tools at our disposal.

Subsets Within Your Broader Vocabulary

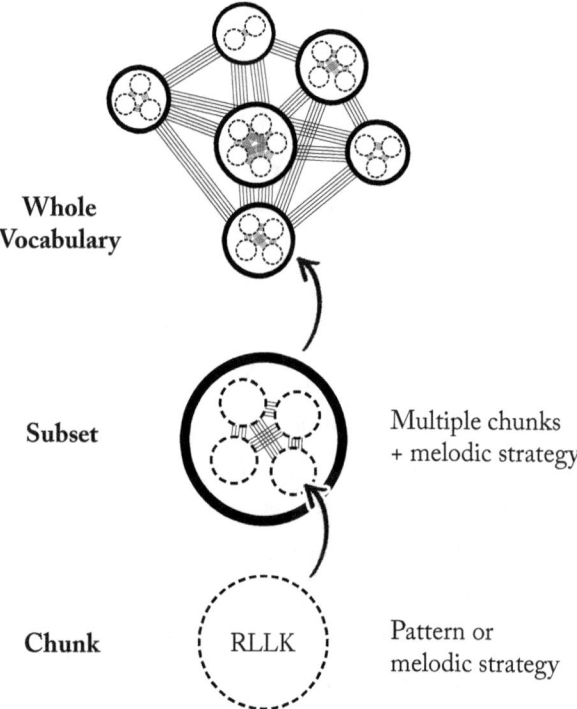

Whole Vocabulary

Subset — Multiple chunks + melodic strategy

Chunk — RLLK — Pattern or melodic strategy

The Web of Drumming Memory

To start, let's look at a common model of human memory to help us visualize our drumming vocabulary. Long-term memory is often conceptualized as a web where items get grouped together according to similarity and relevance.[4c] Let's borrow this basic model and imagine that each node of the web of your drumming memory represents something you can play, while each strand of the web represents your ability to move seamlessly between the two items it connects.

To give us a starting place, the following image represents a hypothetical drummer's improvisation vocabulary:

A Hypothetical Drummer's Improvisation Vocabulary

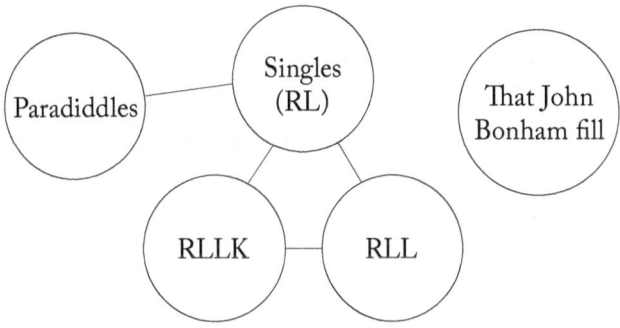

Notice that singles, the RLL pattern, and the RLLK pattern are all connected, meaning that this drummer can move between these to some degree. The RLL pattern is not connected with paradiddles, meaning that it is difficult to move between these two rudiments without breaking the flow of time. Because "That John Bonham fill" was learned in isolation, and exists as muscle memory, it is not yet understood how it can be combined with any of the other elements. Also, notice that different nodes are remembered in different ways, further complicating things. The rudiments are stored as (declarative) stickings, but the John Bonham fill is known only by *sounds like* and *feels like*, and is thus stored only in procedural memory. The fact that each element is not understood in the same way is one reason that moving between them might be difficult, which is another benefit of "thinking in melodies" across the board.

This hypothetical drummer would have a hard time improvising. Some of the rudiments are tenuously connected, but it is not clear which ones work well together. The rudiments themselves may be well understood, but the connections between them are not. Your brain is an association-making machine, but it needs help forming more intentional associations, as opposed to happenstance ones.

Similarity and Relevance

In daily life, you encounter an enormous amount of information on an hourly basis. One way that your brain helps you make sense of this information is by automatically associating things that are similar and relevant.[4d] If you bring to mind your home, a vast web of home-related memories activates. This does not mean that you immediately remember everything at once, but that the nodes of the web are primed so that they are recalled more easily. Moving from one idea on this web to another happens easily, virtually automatically, because the various rooms and items in your home are so tightly associated. For example, if you visualize your front door, you are likely to then visualize the room behind the door, and the act of opening the door. All senses are involved. You might imagine the feeling of turning your doorknob, the sound of the door creaking, or the smell of your entryway. Spontaneous images might appear in mind, like your bed, your kitchen table, or the view from your window. Now that the web is active, if I say the word, "food," you are very likely, of all the infinite food-related things that exist, to think of your own kitchen, and maybe even specific snacks you always keep in your cabinet. The most important thing to notice about this experience is that you were able to remember a huge amount of information with virtually zero effort because each idea is connected to several adjacent ideas, which were preemptively primed by the activation of the web as a whole.

This is a natural and unavoidable feature of human memory, so let's use it to our advantage. We want to create webs of relevance like your home, but for drumming. You might already be thinking of groups of drumming items that are naturally bound by similarity or relevance. To start with the idea of *similarity*, the 4 Paradiddles from the Building Blocks Approach are a good example because they are in fact similar. Another example is flam rudiments—if you spend a few weeks practicing several flam rudiments, you will notice that they all get stored in memory together. As a result, when you suddenly think about playing one flam rudiment, you remember the rest of them too.

Your mind also groups things by *relevance*. For example, when I think about sushi, I also think about soy sauce—not because they are similar, but because they are compatible. Likewise, when I think about punk rock drum beats, I also think about playing singles as fills—not technically similar, but musically compatible.

Although similarity and relevance often go together (because similar patterns have a similar musical aesthetic), relevance is more important for our purposes because we need it in order to *actively* build a web of drumming material. This is different from your memories of home, which form passively. What matters is that we find patterns that work well together, regardless of whether they are technically similar or not. Let's build on an example from the previous chapter— the Down-Up Method using groups of 4 and 2. Our 4 pattern is RLLK, and our 2 pattern is RL. When we randomize these on the fly, it results in a Down-Up Melody played with the right hand, which is why we called it the "4-2 Down-Up." To integrate this 4 pattern and 2 pattern as tightly as possible, we want to understand their compatibility in all of the 5 Ways of Understanding.

Let's start with the measure-long pattern, 44242, which you can see on the next page. It is natural to start by thinking in *stickings*, and get the basic mechanics going. Then we can pay attention to the *counting*, and see which counts are accented. Since our right hand is playing the strong melody note in these patterns, our *notation* will be the melody of the right hand. To start developing *sounds like*, we notice the downs and ups of the melody and sing along. *Feels like* comes from simply repeating it until the coordination is effortless.

Integrating RLLK and RL with an
Example Melody (44242)

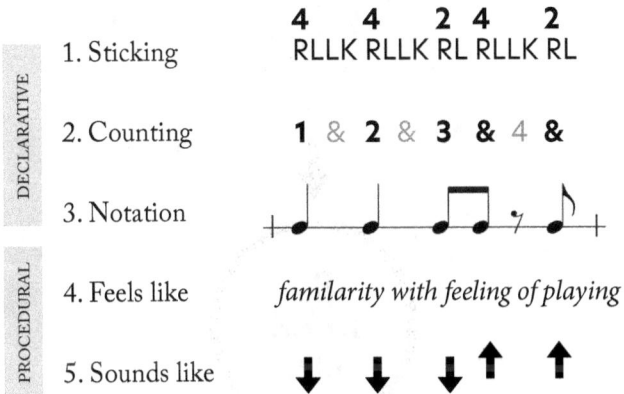

DECLARATIVE	1. Sticking	**4 4 2 4 2** RLLK RLLK RL RLLK RL
	2. Counting	**1** & **2** & **3** **&** 4 **&**
	3. Notation	
PROCEDURAL	4. Feels like	*familarity with feeling of playing*
	5. Sounds like	

This is just one example of a 4-2 Down-Up melody (44242). Let's imagine you continue practicing several others (42424, 42442, 24424, etc.), as well as two-measure examples. And you learn each one with a balance of the 5 Ways. To return to our web metaphor, you can now imagine that each additional way of understanding adds another connecting strand between the two patterns. As you continue drilling them, they eventually become practically fused. At this point, randomizing the 4 and the 2 becomes so effortless that the whole 4-2 Down-Up starts to be recalled as a single item. Now, you can simply "turn on" the 4-2 Down-Up and an unfolding melody with those pieces of vocabulary will flow out effortlessly.

RLLK and RL Merge Into a Subset:

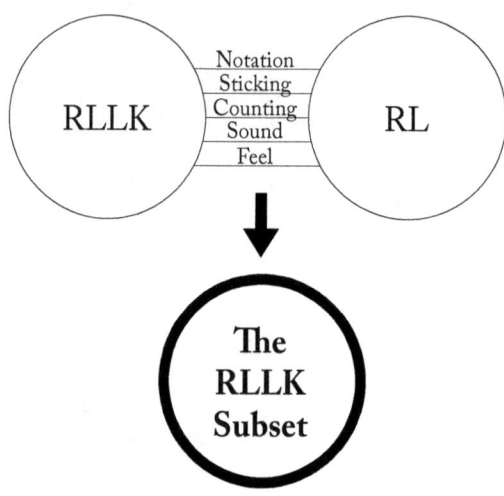

When multiple pieces of vocabulary are made hyper-relevant through a process like this, they form what I call a *subset of vocabulary*. The reason this way of representing your vocabulary is useful is because it closely reflects the subjective experience of playing it. In our metaphorical web, the "RLLK Subset," with all its declarative and procedural information, takes the space of a single item in the web of your drumming memory—a drawer of drawers—and thus feels like a single task. Let's visualize this in our hypothetical drummer's vocabulary from the beginning of this chapter. Now we can add a bolded node that represents a subset.

The RLLK Subset In the
Hypothetical Drummer's Vocabulary

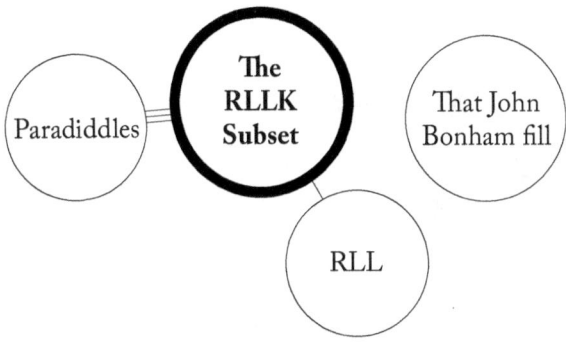

Subsets and the Comfort Zone

The RLLK Subset is our first subset, and it is comprised of three things—two compatible patterns and a melodic strategy for rearranging them on the fly. This reveals the first benefit of subsets: they provide a way of integrating scattered existing vocabulary in a way that enables you to improvise with it. You might have already known the RLLK pattern, singles (RL), and the Down-Up Method, but they were not yet creatively useful in combination. Including a melodic strategy gave us a way of actively strengthening the connection between the patterns until they were permanently bound, while also giving us a way of playing them in an unfolding melody.

When a subset becomes integrated to the point of effortlessness like described above, what you have is a small but important *Comfort Zone*, which consists of the vocabulary that you understand deeply and can improvise with effortlessly.

Comfort Zone vs. Isolated Vocabulary

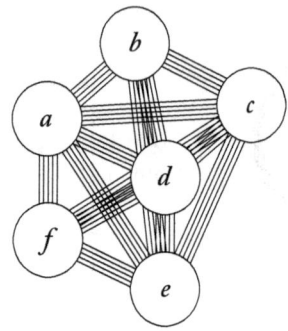

Densely connected
Comfort Zone vocabulary

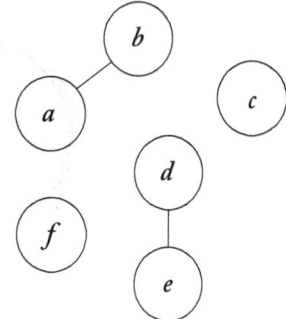

Several isolated
ideas/stickings/memories

The Comfort Zone is crucial for learning new vocabulary and committing it to memory more permanently.

Retention

A new piece of vocabulary threatens us with a very discouraging scenario—when you suddenly realize that something you spent many hours learning two weeks ago is forgotten and you can no longer play it. We can start to intuit a solution to this problem by noticing what a new, isolated piece of vocabulary is missing in our model. It is missing attachments. It is not integrated in a web of relevance, nor a tightly-bound subset. It is "that John Bonham Fill" from our hypothetical vocabulary, or the "double ratamacue" rudiment you were told to practice but were not told why, or that 32-note chop you learned from a video online. When you learn something in isolation (without connections and relevance), it is quickly forgotten because your brain is not designed to remember a thousand little bits of isolated drumming. Instead, we know that it is designed to prime entire webs of relevant drumming all at once, the nodes of which suggest each other with paths you have paved through repetition and traveled down thousands of times before.

Therefore, in order to make a new piece of vocabulary permanent, we need to attach it to a subset in your Comfort Zone that you frequently activate and let the fact that you frequently activate it do the work of cementing the new vocabulary in memory. This loosely imitates a memorization technique called the "Memory Palace" where you take a list of things you want to memorize and visualize placing each of the items in a sequence of specific locations in your home. Once you form these associations, you imagine walking through that sequence of locations, where you "find" all of the items you "left behind."[7] This is one way that people do things like memorize thousands of digits of *pi*. (you associate each number 0-9 with an item, then leave those items around the house). Because the network of memories representing your home has become unforgettable through years of reactivation, and because you have attached this new information to that web in a very detailed way, the new information is there waiting for you when you activate your deeply engrained "home web."

The drumming equivalent of the Memory Palace is your *Comfort Zone* vocabulary, which, like your memory of home, is deeply engrained in memory to the point of being unforgettable, and is part of your daily drumming existence. Attaching new drumming chunks and subsets to your existing, deeply familiar, and effortless Comfort Zone helps them become permanent. It also helps them become immediately useful because you are attaching them as creative additions to patterns you already like using. The main difference is that the standard Memory Palace deals with declarative memory (numbers, playing cards, etc.), while the Comfort Zone deals with procedural memory too (drumming). Let's see how it works in an example where we attach a new piece of vocabulary (the paradiddle-diddle) to our existing Comfort Zone.

Imagine that you encounter a short lesson online where someone is teaching "An INSANE Chop!!" The sticking on the screen is: RLRRLLRLRRLLRLRL. You, having read this book, immediately think two things. First, the psychology class chunking example, XNSAFBICIAX, comes to mind, and you identify that this is too many individual items to remember. You need chunks. You notice that the teacher is using paradiddle-diddles (PDD) the sticking for which is RLRRLL, and you see four singles at the end (RLRL), so all 32 of those R's and L's can be reduced to "PDD + PDD + 4."

The second thing you realize is that we are missing a melodic strategy. This is just a single one-measure fill. You can learn it, sure, but what are the chances you are going to need *this* one-measure fill specifically? If you spend all day practicing this fill, you will have learned it in an airtight container where it will always live detached from anything else in your vocabulary. In two weeks, if you remember it, it will not be available in the midst of improvisation. Because your goal is fluent improvisation, you are not interested in learning a single insane chop, rather you want to develop the ability to improvise using the elements that make up said insane chop. Since the RLLK Subset is our newly-established Comfort Zone, let's see how we can attach the PDD to it.

The paradiddle-diddle is a group of six notes (RLRRLL), so we recognize that it will fit well into the 4-2 Down-Up, where we constantly play 4's and 2's in combination, and which is part of our budding Comfort Zone. I always advise students to start by jumping into the deep end when they encounter a new exercise: get your RLLK Subset going and try throwing in PDD's on the fly. Sometimes, and progressively more frequently as your vocabulary expands, you will find that you can just do it. For now, let's assume that is not the case. Therefore, even though we are dealing with your effortless Comfort Zone, you need to add constraints that reduce the complexity back down into a creative exercise that is simple enough to master, and which targets this new vocabulary. In fact, you might even need to go back a step further and spend time with technical drills that build the basic coordination and melodic familiarity with the new pattern. You dig out those 4-2 melodies that you originally used to build the RLLK Subset (42442, 44242, 42424, etc.) and look at all the places you could substitute a 6 (PDD) for a 4+2 or a 2+4. You run the drills until they are easy. Then you turn to creative exercises where you practice rearranging 2's, 4's, and 6's on the fly without referencing the previous exercises.

You set the constraints tightly at first, and slowly expand until you are back to your original level of effortlessness. Since the PDD is now attached to your Comfort Zone, which you frequently reactivate when playing, it becomes a permanent part of your improvisation vocabulary.

This might sound like a lot of work, but you are going to master the drills and creative exercises more quickly this time around because the core coordination and melodic familiarity is already established. Furthermore, like we did when we justified spending four months on creative exercises for passing the soccer ball, consider the gains. You have just integrated one of the most common and useful rudiments in all of drumming into your vocabulary in a way that makes it virtually unforgettable and musically useful. What is two months of practice in exchange for a lifetime of creative utility? For the rest of your life, instead of constantly brushing up on it as an isolated exercise and subsequently forgetting it again, you can start to experiment with orchestration and dynamic variations, like you did with RLLK and RL. As you build variations on top of the original pattern, the original pattern becomes even easier, even more deeply understood, and even more well integrated. It becomes permanent.

A New Subset From Scratch

With the paradiddle-diddle, we were lucky that it worked so well with our RLLK Subset, but what happens when you want to integrate something that does not fit well with anything else in your vocabulary? What if it was a triplet pattern and your entire Comfort Zone was in straight time? Since the maxim of this chapter is *learn nothing in isolation*, the answer is to build an entire new subset around it. This is not as substantial a task as it sounds. Remember, subsets start small. The RLLK Subset started as two patterns and a melodic strategy. You already have all the tools and know all the steps. Let's walk through two examples.

For the first example, let's take a triplet pattern like mentioned above. Let's say that you have always loved playing the 6-stroke roll in triplets, the sticking of which is RLLRRL. You are comfortable playing the pattern, but as soon as you try to combine it with other triplet material, it falls apart. Let's replicate the process we took to build our RLLK Subset. Instead of a 4, we need a 6. Instead of a 2, we need a 3. Our 6 pattern is RLLRRL. Our 3 pattern can be RLL. First step: drills. Instead of rearranging 4's and 2's, you rearrange 6's and 3's (66363, 63663, 63636, 36636, 36366, etc.). These create down-up melodies just like the 4's and 2's did, so we will call it the "6-3 Down-Up." Second step: creative exercises. You start rearranging 6's and 3's on the fly and find, since you are becoming a Down-Up Method expert, that this step comes quickly. Voilà, you just created a subset around your 6-stroke roll. You can play an unfolding melody with control by moving between these super useful and common patterns. If you revisit this frequently for a few weeks until it become effortless, you might even start to call this your triplet Comfort Zone.

For a second example, let's take the pattern, RLK, in straight 16th notes, and develop a subset around it. Up to this point, all the patterns in our straight-time Comfort Zone are made of even numbers (2, 4, and 6), so if we add a group of 3 it will displace everything by one 16th note. This is possible, but it is very difficult, so you decide instead to build the RLK pattern a subset of its own. This will require a completely different approach than either of the last two examples.

First, you do the drills that help you loop RLK indefinitely in straight time. A group of three does not land on Beat 1 again until three bars later, which is an awkward phrase length, so you loop just the first bar, then just the second, then just the third. Then you loop two bars at a time. Eventually, you drill your way to looping the pattern without losing track of Beat 1. The first thing that is different about this subset is that you do not need a melodic strategy. Looping groups of three in straight time *is* an unfolding melody. It is called "dotted 8th notes," and since it creates a polyrhythm, the melody automatically changes from measure to measure, which is something we cannot say about looping the RLLK pattern or the triplet 6-stroke roll.

Now we are looping the RLK pattern, and it is giving us an unfolding melody, though a very repetitive one. For phase two, we build variation by using different accent-ghost combinations with the hands. First, you accent both hands. Then you ghost both hands. Then you accent the right hand and ghost the left. Then you accent the left and ghost the right. Now you have four accent variations. Your goal with this creative exercise is to get to the point where you can randomize the accent variations while looping RLK.

The unique thing about this subset is that it only contains one pattern. Since the RLK pattern constantly shifts itself through the bar, adding these dynamic options on top of the already-shifting pattern results in an explosion of melodic variation. Like with all the other subsets, you could then explore additional, related patterns (RL, RK, RLKK, RLLK, RRLK, RRLLK, etc.). That would continue to be creatively fruitful, but the point here is that we have already crossed the tipping point for considering this a subset that offers a large amount of improvisational freedom, and you have made the RLK pattern into a permanent memory.

Imagine that you have done this work and feel confident improvising within each of your three subsets: RLLK Subset, 6-Stroke Roll Subset, and RLK Subset. Before charging ahead, we can take a moment to notice a subtle benefit that we are gaining. By adding structure to how we conceptualize our vocabulary, we give ourselves a way to take stock and keep track of what we know. Instead of 30 disparate ideas, we have three subsets of vocabulary, the contents of which we know intimately. This helps us when anxiety makes our minds go blank on stage. When your nerves are preventing you from just "letting it flow," it will be useful to be able to reference a declarative mental map, so that you can consciously and intentionally choose from a known stock of subsets.

Now, at last, we have paved our way to the most powerful creative tool in this book, which also gets us very close to an answer to our guiding question: *what does it feel like to improvise?*

Moving Between Subsets

Creative exercises initially helped us effortlessly move between individual patterns to form subsets. Now we will use creative exercises to learn to effortlessly move between entire subsets. Since you can now do controlled improvisation *within* each subset, we want to structure creative exercises that help you move *between* them without being overwhelmed by the possibilities. We previously saw how learning two isolated patterns does not mean you will suddenly be able to rearrange them on the fly. Likewise, mastering two subsets does not mean you will suddenly feel comfortable moving between them either. Relying on the same principles laid out in Chapter 4 (*Practicing Improvisation*), we can come up with creative exercises that use constraints to build the coordination and the mental tools that help us start improvising with *all* our vocabulary.

Let's start by taking two compatible subsets we have already talked about—the RLLK Subset ("Subset A") and the RLK Subset ("Subset B"). Since *control* must always be our goal, let's begin with a very simple structure: alternate between four measures improvising with Subset A and four measures with Subset B, without breaking the flow of 16th notes. The transition points are where you will initially encounter problems. You will find that one or two notes need to be changed, added, or cut short as you transition, and your intuition for solving those problems in real time will start to develop. As we know, this means you are starting to develop *the glue*. Eventually, we reduce it to two measures of each, then one measure of each. This is a solid start, but this will always sound blocky. Ultimately, we want to be able to switch at any point in the measure, and maybe only momentarily. So, our next step is to target less obvious moments for switching. Below are four examples of how you could practice moving between the subsets. Each one is its own creative exercise that helps you develop your bar awareness and your glue.

Practicing Moving Between Subsets

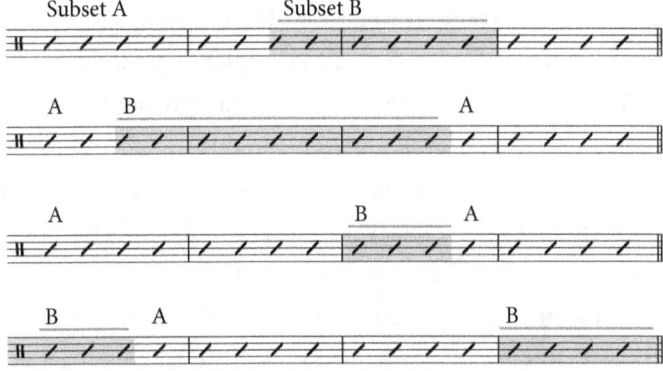

Now we are improvising both within subsets as well as between subsets. Though I am presenting the "between subsets" level as a next step, you ultimately move back and forth between these two levels fluidly as you practice. While you are working at the "between subsets" level, you might notice that a specific pattern within one subset is causing you trouble. You can then switch to the "within subset" level and come up with a few creative exercises that help iron out the issue before returning to the "between subsets" level. You might also move down to the "within subset" level to add a new pattern or orchestration. If the new pattern is challenging in itself, this might even mean moving down to the pattern level and simply drilling the coordination, independence, or speed. As you expand your options within each subset, the musical possibilities that result from moving between subsets exponentially grows.

The way you practice moving between three or even four subsets at the same time follows the same process. For example, you could introduce a triplet-based subset that works at the same tempo, like your triplet 6-stroke subset, in which case your creative exercises need to account for all three subsets. You could cycle through the three of them, or you could place the triplet subset on one side of the switch and both straight time subsets on the other. You will find over time that multiple compatible subsets that you frequently train together slowly merge into one, giving you a subset of subsets. This happens when moving between those subsets becomes so effortless that they start to feel like one item in your mind. Like we have seen before, as switching between subsets becomes easier, this frees up more mental space to think genuinely creative thoughts.

Subsets as a Creative Tool

Moving between subsets is a creative tool that is as powerful as it is simple. Once you establish two or more subsets, you can strategically jump between them to leverage the musical characteristics of both and create higher-order musical effects like contrast, surprise, or tension and release. This allows you to think about telling a story without stumbling over how to spell and pronounce words along the way. This step epitomizes our maxim, *think simple thoughts, play complex things,* because as the complexity of your drumming increases exponentially, your thinking simplifies to the point where all you need to decide is when to "flip the switch" between subsets.

The musical value that we get from this tool comes from the fact that different subsets have inherently different musical characteristics. One subset might sound smooth and fluid, while another sounds syncopated and jagged. Since these qualities are built into the subsets, and since you can run those subsets automatically, you are left with sufficient mental space to think about how you are going to create movement. If the syncopated subset feels tense, and the smooth one feels comparatively like a release, you might start with the smooth subset, and start sprinkling in more and more of the syncopated subset (building tension) until right at the end of the section when you switch completely to the syncopated material (climax), and then switch back to only the smooth stuff (release). This type of thinking is crucial because it gives your playing movement. Variation for variation's sake will come across as random. The point of developing variation is to create movement because movement is the driving force of musicality.

Likewise, moving between subsets when composing drum parts gives you a simple way to create surprise or contrast from one section to the next. If you are exploring grooves at a writing session with your band, you might leverage two different groove-based subsets—one where your right hand plays intricate melodies over the groove and one where it keeps simple time. You could maintain the same underlying melody while the rules of the subset change from section to section, which would provide both continuity and evolution. There are countless ways you can create movement by leveraging the work you have already automated within various subsets. Expanding the content of existing subsets, building new subsets around isolated vocabulary, and becoming more skilled at moving between subsets will multiply your musical possibilities. Over time, this will lead to you thinking *continually simpler* thoughts, while playing *progressively more complex* things.

So, What Does It Feel Like to Improvise?

To finally hit the nail on the head, we now have everything we need to answer our guiding question. Fluent improvisation often feels like strategically moving between melodic strategies and subsets of vocabulary, each of which is full of musically-related patterns and melodies, the technical execution of which is automated. It feels most often like we are *thinking in melodies*, and that we are mostly making decisions about how to deliver those unfolding melodies to the kit. It feels as though we are supervising a mostly automated team, but that we understand in declarative technical terms what the team is doing so that we can zoom in when needed to guide a specific sticking or melody. It feels that there is great alignment between our physical drumming abilities and our mental representation of drumming.

What is remarkable, and what may continue to make improvisation seem paradoxical to some, is that there is practically no randomness involved. I want to dispel the idea once and for all that improvisation is inventing random drumming in real time. What we have learned about the mind shows us that that is not even possible. Speaking a thought does not feel like randomly selecting from all the words you know. Randomizing the words you know would not be remotely possible because each word exists within a web of relevance that is automatically activated as you speak and thus influences the next word that is spoken. On top of this, the logic and topic of the conversation, as well as the rules of grammar, radically reduce the possible vocabulary options as the sentence progresses, excluding most of the words in the language. Your drumming vocabulary unfolds in a similar way. Coherence depends much more on exclusion than inclusion. Up to this point, all of the methods we have learned in this book have involved radically reducing what you allow yourself to play. When we improvise, we move constantly not between individual items, but between deeply integrated webs, chunks, and groupings of ideas. This is not only what makes improvisation possible, it is what gives it coherence to both you and your listener.

Let's take it all one step further. We have seen the recurring tendency of your mind to create stronger and stronger links between things that are frequently mixed together. We leveraged this at the pattern level, the subset level, and the between-subset level, but it also applies one level higher at the level of musical strategy. What we described above with the syncopated and smooth subsets was a loose pattern for moving between two subsets to create tension and release within a section. As long as one subset feels more tense, and the other feels comparatively like a release, the pacing of the switching—the musical strategy—will be musically effective even if you change out the subsets for different ones. Over time, musical strategies that you find effective become deeply engrained in memory as well, mostly at the level of intuition. Like we said of the dancer automating grace (if they move at all, it is beautiful), we can say of you as a drummer that, at this point, you are automating *musicality*. If you drum, beatbox, or merely tap on the table, it is good music.

The Russian Doll of Creative Automation

We now have multiple layers of creative variation, all operating simultaneously and mostly automatically, nested within each other like a Russian doll of creative automation. At the pattern level, we automated stickings and chunked various dynamic and orchestration options. At the subset level, we used melodic strategies to effortlessly create continually-varying melodies. At the between-subset level, we automated the act of moving between complex subsets at any point in a measure. And now, at the musical strategy level, we automated patterns of switching between subsets that are musically effective. Your Creative Director supervises this process from a listening position as all of the layers function simultaneously. You zoom in to this or that level as needed, but, at this point, they can often sit back and simply appreciate the efficiency, complexity, and musicality of your playing.

All the way back in Chapter 2, we talked about the master drummer who tells us that they are not thinking anything when they play. I said that this was not helpful for us at the time, but that it was true nonetheless, and that we would eventually understand this as a reflection of the depth of that drummer's mastery. Here we are. When you see your favorite drummer play a musical, dynamic, captivating solo, and then they tell you that they just opened the faucet and let it flow, you can now appreciate how deeply trained all of these interdependent layers of creative automation are.

We can also understand clearly now why drummers who improvise masterfully seem so energized and look like they are having so much fun (look up a video of Chris Coleman to see the joy of improvisational mastery). We saw this with riding a bike, with soccer, and with all our creative exercises. Games are fun because they are engaging and challenging, and they demand that you creatively navigate difficult but manageable problems in the moment. We saw how, in drumming, this steady stream of challenges comes not from an opponent but from the act of forming novel combinations while being tethered to the passing time.

With increasing mastery—which means adding more patterns, more combinations, more subsets, more strategies, more speed, more orchestration options, etc.—the challenge of the game increases, but so does your ability to play it. You establish control over and over again every day that you push the boundary. What eventually and inevitably emerges from playing a game at such a high level of mastery is *beauty*—not just in the music but also in the sheer fluency of the act of creation. This is why the journey is worth taking, and it is why I never shy away from teaching people how to play the drums alone.

Drumming Alone

By now, you may have noticed that this whole book is about playing the drums alone. This might seem strange, given that the drums are typically thought of as an accompanying instrument. The reason for this is twofold. First, this is a book for all drummers, particularly non-professional and aspiring professionals. For the vast majority of us, at least 95% of our drumming takes place in the practice room, alone. Even for those who join bands or go on to enjoy quite a busy gigging schedule, the fact of the matter is that musical opportunities come and go. Some are creatively rewarding, and many are not. At the end of the day, or the end of the decade, or the end of your career, you will always come back to your drum set, in your basement, in your rehearsal space, in your garage, and sit down with it one-on-one, like an old friend, to pick up the conversation where you left off. If you can make that time more fulfilling, then you are adding something significant and positive to your life.

So, you could call that the practical reason, but the other, more important, reason is that I want to emphasize that developing a fulfilling study of an instrument is *enough*. Pursuing a career in music is certainly worthwhile for those interested, and can be rewarding in many ways, but it is just that—a career. It is a unique career in that you might have an opportunity to be a part of something magical from time to time, but it also includes its fair share of tedium and unsentimental "jobs," not to mention its fair share of struggles and anxiety. The point is that the magic is still available to you whether or not you have made music your career. When you develop a fulfilling relationship with your instrument, you create a robust source of creativity that contributes to your well-being in general. If I were never going to perform again, I would still go to my rehearsal space and play my drums. You are going to spend hundreds, maybe thousands of hours developing the skill of fluent improvisation. To fortify the patience and commitment that this will require of you, let's spend one final chapter together pondering the question: *why bother?*

Chapter Terms

- **Subset:** A natural way of organizing your vocabulary. Made up of multiple patterns or variations that have been made hyper-compatible. Offers enough variety for improvisation.

- **Your Comfort Zone:** The vocabulary you can improvise with effortlessly. Requires little attention. Your "home."

- **Retention:** Improves when new vocabulary is integrated with an existing, commonly used subset. Alternatively, build a new subset around new vocabulary. Learn nothing in isolation.

- **Moving Between Subsets:** A way of exponentially increasing the complexity and musicality of your improvisation. A crucial creative tool.

Chapter 7

Why Bother?

If you made it to this final chapter, it seems safe to assume that for you, like me, drumming really matters. You might feel that it plays a role in keeping you sane, that it connects you to something bigger than yourself, or that it brings you joy, pride, or even peace of mind. It might have facilitated some of your most cherished friendships and memories, or be your ticket into a flow state that grounds you after a stressful day. However, for all the wonderful contributions an instrument can make to your life, it is far too easy *not* to notice them, and instead remain eternally fixated on the current thing you *cannot* do in the practice room, with all the frustration and hopelessness that comes with it. To miss the forest for the trees in this way is like going to church every week and stressing about whether or not you pronounce the words in the hymns perfectly—it misses the point entirely. You are already in the lucky position of having a hobby that can be deeply rewarding, creative, meditative, and even spiritually valuable, so let's make sure we have the right frame of mind to notice the benefits we are already reaping and cultivate the ones we are not. In this chapter, we will take stock of all the positive things drumming adds to your life other than the literal drumming. We will move from the pragmatic and expected to the profound and possibly magical, starting with something so obvious that you might never have noticed it at all—drumming is a pillar of your private life.

Have a Private Life

Your private life is many things. It is everything you do outside of your "professional life" and your "social media life." It excludes the former because work is usually obligatory, and the latter because online life is a sort of performance. Your private life is unselfconscious, authentic, and, for some, spiritual and creative. Given the necessity of work and the allure of social media, perhaps what one's private life is most of all, however, is *forgotten*. Mixing up your private life with your professional life and social media life has a tendency to ruin the things that are supposed to bring you the most joy, which is something I know from personal experience as well as from countless students and peers in the music industry.

When I was immersed in social media in my early twenties, I broadcasted everything onto the internet from both my professional life and what should have been my private life. This had the effect of blurring the lines between what I did for myself and what I did to entertain or impress other people. The anxiety of my career and the weird incentives of social media bled into my private life constantly. In this state of general self-consciousness, I remember the advice, "Have a private life," striking me as a revelation. I understood what it meant to have a successful professional life—I was obsessed with developing one—but what did it mean to have a fulfilling private life?

As my music career became more routine, and therefore began to resemble just another job, I began to sense that something fundamental was lacking: I had no private life. I did nothing for its own sake, nothing for myself, and nothing carefree. Everything was tied to some extrinsic goal and, when left alone, I didn't know what to do with myself, so I just worked more. With all my well-being eggs in one basket—one that was too closely tied to other people's opinions of me and whether I had gigs coming in—my well-being crumbled quickly when work wasn't going well, and my relationship with drumming started losing its joy.

I see this happen often with students when they become too wrapped up in the awful incentives of broadcasting their drumming to social media. I remind them how much fun they used to have when they played the drums just for themselves, and I encourage them to keep all or most of their drumming for their private lives (unselfconscious, authentic, for its own sake) instead of their social media lives or professional lives (performative, self-conscious, externally validated).

A fulfilling private life is one full of valuable hobbies, relationships, and interests. It is a way of diversifying your well-being portfolio, so that when a single pillar is shaken, your whole world doesn't come crumbling down. If you chose to read this book, then drumming is probably one of the pillars of your private life—a sustainable source of meaning, stability, and joy, and something you'll do for its own sake for the rest of your life. It may seem strange for a professional drummer, but in order to sustain a healthy relationship with my drums, I had to start seeing them again as a hobby first and a career second. You can lose a job, but no one can fire you from your private life.

Passion Is Overrated

People who want to inspire you don't usually tell you to develop a hobby. They tend to use the word *passion* a lot. "Find your passion and pursue it," they say. "Since your passion is so inspiring, with a little hard work you're bound to succeed." These people are always suspiciously driven and energetic. The first problem with this advice is that *passion* carries with it the unrealistic expectation that doing the work will be easy, or fun, or energizing, and not at all tedious. In reality, of the ten thousand hours one is supposed to spend developing mastery, the majority of mine were spent tinkering away, often exhausted, often resisting (or succumbing to) the urge to call it quits early. If I factor in the anxiety surrounding performances, regular discouragements, financial insecurity, feelings of inadequacy or envy, and the outright drudgery of lugging a fifty-pound hardware bag around Boston and New York, the word *passion* seems to hardly capture the experience. Don't get me wrong, there is plenty of joy, and the special moments make it worth it, but I fear that so much passion-talk convinces people that they do not like the things they love as much as they think they do. Things that are worth doing are not always fun or easy. It is the subtle satisfaction of dedication and the hard-won steps of real progress that drive you forward more than any exuberant feeling of passion. If you are not leaping out of bed and racing to the practice room, you might easily conclude that you are "not passionate" about the drums after all. But that's OK because passion is simply the wrong metric.

The truism, "Passion fades," is no less applicable to your hobbies than your relationships, but the end of the infatuation phase is a positive sign because it means you are moving on to a more mature type of love. Your goal is to be the 80-year-old couple quietly and adorably holding hands that I just saw on the subway today—but with your drums. No one would mistake the absence of passion in that scene for an absence of really deep love, something sustainable and beautiful. The trick to loving the drums is accepting that there will be ups and downs as you patiently develop your relationship with them. If curiosity, interest, or some *je ne sais quoi* invariably draws you back to the drums, that's *enough*. That's a sign that you really like them. You might even love them. And *that* is the root of a lifelong hobby.

This brings us to my second gripe with the follow-your-passion talk: passion can be *developed*. Searching for a hobby that is always thrilling and never tedious is like searching for a soul mate with whom you never disagree or have conflict. Often, it is not until you get quite deep into learning about something (or someone) that you realize how rewarding and sustainable it could be. This is why it is so important not to corrupt your hobby's incentives from the very beginning by immediately broadcasting your progress to the internet. Keep those dreams of YouTube stardom far, far away, and just see if you can develop a healthy relationship with your instrument first. If something keeps bringing you back to the drums, and that thing isn't your desire for views and likes, then you're probably looking at a sustainable hobby, and that hobby might be something that brings you joy for the rest of your life.

The Value of Hobbies

To continue this train of thought, valuable hobbies are much more important than people think. To fill your private life with one or multiple worthwhile hobbies is to protect yourself from the most addictive and meaningless traps of mass society. If you have nothing that interests you deeply, nothing to pick up today where you left off yesterday, nothing that is self-driven and self-dependent, then infinite-entertainment and boredom-induced doomscrolling make it remarkably easy to waste countless hours in ways that you regret.

In this sense, the benefits of valuable hobbies are twofold. They add value at the same time that they protect against what is dangerous. Regarding what they add, a hobby is a vehicle for experiencing some of the most rewarding things in life— to name just a few: facing fears and challenges, setting and accomplishing meaningful goals, meeting new people and making friends, teaching others what you know, and finding a creative outlet. Furthermore, the more proficient you become at something, the easier it becomes to find and create new opportunities, which creates a snowball effect of growth.

One of my favorite parts of a good hobby is the joy of the "private victory." You know you're doing something for the right reason when you have a breakthrough and you don't even need to tell anyone about it because the victory is sufficient in itself. Often, you're so deep down a rabbit hole at that point that it would be hard to explain to someone why the breakthrough even matters to you. This is why the idea of having a "relationship with" your hobby feels right. So many things that are genuinely important to you are destined to be shared between only you and your drums.

Hobbies sound lighthearted, but for some people there can be a profound, even existential, side to all of this. To consciously choose and pursue long-term interests is to claim responsibility for fostering your growth and to take ownership of the person you become, as opposed to being shaped by happenstance. Everywhere you look in the history of good advice, you find some version of "know yourself," which is something you cannot do if you do not exercise *your* curiosity and pursue what you care about in a way that only you can. To persist in activities that enable you to make discoveries through your own effort, the benefits of which only you can truly appreciate, and the result of which you find beautiful or rewarding, is to discover and form yourself.

Your Social Life

Another benefit of hobbies is that they offer opportunities to form meaningful relationships. Feeling like you are a part of something larger than yourself protects against loneliness. Drumming will not make you a social butterfly, but it can create numerous opportunities for you to leave your cocoon, and it is worth noticing them. To name a few, becoming a proficient drummer enables you to join the band at school or church, attend or organize a weekly jam, frequent the local drum shop to shoot the breeze, play in the pit orchestra of a local musical, organize a local masterclass, or start a band of your own.

One of the best things about having hobbies is that it makes it easier to find fellow enthusiasts who are excited to become friends. During the various times that my parents have moved, my mother, who is a great musician, always found that music was her way of integrating into a new community. One thing I learned from her was never to let shyness prevent me from taking the first step. You'd be amazed how little resistance you encounter when you just start organizing people to do things. This is because most people would *love* to participate in projects with other like-minded people, but everyone is afraid to make the first move. Be the one who initiates. I sometimes feel that half of the success in my career has been due to the simple fact that I never hesitate to be the guy that gets the ball rolling.

For aspiring professionals, these types of community connections are the types of things you start to build a budding career on. Even if you later decide to move to another city, what you will have taught yourself is how to find and create opportunities for yourself and others. If you also happen to be a decent drummer, that is a potent combination for success no matter where you are.

And then, of course, there are other drummers to connect with. The most resoundingly positive feedback from students who have chosen to attend multi-day drum camps is that they make a handful of drum friends and form a group online where they can celebrate their victories, commiserate over their struggles, and encourage one another. Many people who join educational websites like mine feel surprisingly deep accountability and comradery with their fellow students in the online forum. Attending a summer program or going to music school is likely to produce at least a couple of lifelong friends and a network of like-minded peers. It is also possible that over time you will start to feel a sense of belonging in the broader drum community, and perhaps even the drum community of the past.

Ancient Friends

History was never of much interest to me growing up, the history of drums least of all. However, when I returned to school at 28-years-old in search of a more classic academic experience, something about my philosophy course struck me. When I found ancient philosophers asking some of the same questions I tended to ask myself, which are some of the same questions we are addressing even in this chapter of the book, I was surprised to notice that it gave me a subtle sense of belonging and comfort. To know that this ancient person had experiences similar to mine, and that we sometimes followed the same trains of thought to similar conclusions, felt like I was getting a faint glimpse of human nature. It added the dimension of time to the idea of community. People often emphasize that the utility of studying history is to avoid making historically doomed decisions, but I had never experienced how the study of history itself can offer a sense of belonging. I suppose I am merely describing the feeling that serves as the basis of tradition. This is another commonplace idea that I was taking for granted, which only needed recognizing in order to bring more meaning into several parts of life.

If you are able to see yourself as the inheritor of generations of drumming innovation, instead of just one of a million drummers in the present moment, you might develop the feeling that you are part of the greater unfolding lineage of those who have studied and contributed to this art form. This makes drumming less of a competition and more of a family tradition. Consider how religious services, the prototype of tradition, usually include reading wise words written long ago, appreciating their wisdom, and trying to integrate them into your life. Observe how similar this is to us sitting with an old record and appreciating the innovation and wisdom in a legend's playing before spending time trying to integrate their tools or philosophy into our own playing. After enough recitation, we hear echoes of their work coming from our own hands, adapting to the music of the present, and bringing us more deeply into the art.

Appreciating Music More Deeply

An accomplished singer who is a friend of mine recently began learning the drums. As we were walking to my studio for a lesson, she told me that learning the drums had changed what she hears when she listens to music. The experience of listening to music had become enriched and more complex. There was *more to hear*, and therefore, more to think about and appreciate. This, by itself, is one of the greatest benefits of learning an art. There are only a handful of categories of art, and each one of them is a never-ending opportunity to sustain a lifetime of meaningful exploration, learning, and creation. Deepening your study of your instrument allows you to participate in music in a qualitatively different way.

To step outside of music, this applies to pretty much everything. Chess is more interesting to watch if you understand chess strategy. Einstein's theory of relativity is more exciting to someone who gets the math. Romantic poetry means more to someone who understands its historical context. And you appreciate your parents more after you become a parent. Speaking of parents, as a case-in-point, my now-retired father has lately been deepening his religious faith through various study groups. As a result, his experience of the church service—the same one he has attended for decades—has become something completely different. Every moment of the service has become more meaningful, historical, and profound. Likewise, you might find that the experience of practicing and performing drums, even the same patterns and songs you have played your whole life, becomes more fulfilling and meaningful as a result of deepening your study of the instrument.

Music and Your Spiritual Life

I'm determined not to lose any readers in this section. Be warned: we are going to talk about music and spirituality, but we are going to do it without LSD, candles, or music festival tickets. We'll use the same analytical eye we've used for this whole book. You can get as hippy-dippy or not with me in this section, but the point is that we absolutely cannot talk about the benefits of playing drums—the most ancient and common instrument in spiritual practices since the beginning of human history—without noticing this apparent power. For all time, in every corner of the world, people have experienced strikingly similar transformative experiences through music making.[8] In tribal cultures, music, and specifically drumming, is a common feature of consciousness-altering spiritual ceremonies.[9] To play the drums your whole life without taking stock of this is to miss something important. Music plays a role in every spiritual practice and can be a part of your spiritual life regardless of your beliefs.

It's hard to deny that there is something intangible and mystical-feeling about music, but this can be explained by understanding some ways that music is unique from other art forms. First, let's focus on music without lyrics. To start by stating what seems obvious, this type of music does not rely on language or visual stimuli. Every other art form does. The reason this is significant is that language and vision are the primary tools we use to make sense of our everyday experience. Every moment we are awake, we automatically, pre-consciously process the world with language and vision, reflexively categorizing and associating objects and ideas. We receive and communicate ideas using language. Even our thinking—our inner dialogue—functions largely through language. Language and vision help us keep track of things by making them into "items" in our minds.

Though sound is obviously a part of most waking experiences, it is only in the realm of music where it is detached from language and vision and made the sole substance of the experience. Poetry, literature, theater, and film, which can evoke emotions as strong or stronger than music, do so to a significant degree with language and narrative. Even when language is being used in a way that is abstract and metaphorical, the emotions you feel remain to some degree attached to real world things and ideas. When we see someone on the stage, screen, or page suffering, we can identify the source of our emotion narratively and explain with words the connection. In short, we have words for that.

On the other hand, when a series of musical notes passes, they refer to…nothing. They do not activate a web of language and they do not refer directly to any object or idea in the world. In short, we do not have words for that. They exist in themselves as an auditory experience. This in itself isn't good or bad, but the remarkable thing about those passing musical notes is that, despite the fact that they refer to nothing in a literal sense, they can evoke powerful emotions. They still *mean* something to us even though they evade our tools of description.

This is one reason music might be so universally attractive. Psychologically, by not using words, music bypasses the reasoning parts of the brain that think with language, but still "communicates" with subconscious parts of the brain that are involved with pleasure, love, compassion, and empathy. Its ability to evoke emotions without the objects and narratives of the real world gives us the opportunity to "play" in the realm of pure emotion. This means that we can experience the "essence" of an emotion without the consequences that typically accompany it in real life. This might be why it feels good to listen to sad music.[10] Anyone who has had a good cry knows the catharsis caused even by "negative" emotions. Music gives us some of that catharsis even when we aren't going through a hard (or good) time, which means that the raw sensation in your body that we call sadness maybe isn't inherently negative at all. It just tends to occur when unfortunate things are happening to us.

Since our typical experience of the world is through language and vision, this helps us understand why music can feel "otherworldly." The Oxford Dictionary definition of *mystery* is: "something that is difficult or impossible to understand or explain." Part of why music is nearly ubiquitous in spiritual practices is because it is among the experiences that evade our standard tools of explanation. It therefore feels *mystical*, aka, filled with mystery.

Does adding lyrics negate this unique quality in music? In most cases, no. Good lyrics enhance the emotional power of music without reducing its abstract nature too much. This is why most people feel that good lyrics are somewhat ambiguous or abstract—less like literature and more like poetry, where the point is more to evoke feelings that may have little to do with the literal words than it is to recount a series of events. Furthermore, it is telling that the emotional content of the lyrics tends to be overpowered by the emotion of the accompanying music because the music and even the melody of the vocals communicates directly with those subconscious, emotional parts of your brain. Happy lyrics sung over sad music will be felt as sad, not happy. In this way, from an emotional perspective, lyrics are accompaniment to the music, though we tend to think of it the other way around.

This framing helps us think about the unique pull of music in a way that even the spiritual skeptic won't roll their eyes at. Everything we just said, after all, simply describes the basic psychology that we all share when we listen to music. So, the step we just took is to simply notice that our hobby deals with something experientially unique and possibly profound. When we combine this intangible aspect of music with what we know from previous chapters about building layers of automation that enable us to improvise, it primes us to have one of the most seemingly mystical experiences the drums can offer.

Awe

Awe is a fundamental part of spiritual life. Awe happens when we encounter something physically, aesthetically, morally, or spiritually beyond our ability to assimilate it into current mental categories.[11]

It is an essential component of the quintessential "religious experience." Given what we know about the incredible amount of multi-layered automation systematically built into your procedural memory during thousands of hours of creative practice, and given what we just discussed about music's ability to bypass your conscious mind and speak to emotional centers of the brain, we can start to see how our own drumming practice offers an opportunity to regularly experience awe.

In the previous chapter, we showed how it is that the master drummer who says they "just let it happen" can simultaneously be "not thinking" and performing enormously complex drumming. We also discussed how this level of effortless flow is available relatively early on within limited subsets of vocabulary. Once you can open the faucet and effortlessly let drumming flow, the opportunity arises for a simple shift in attention. You now have the opportunity to "watch the show." Of course, you watch yourself play drums every time you practice, but the difference I'm trying to highlight is akin to the difference between breathing like you do all day without noticing and using your breath as a focal point of meditation. As a meditation teacher would instruct you to do with your breathing: bring your attention to your body while you effortlessly improvise and simply notice what is happening. What you find borders on unbelievable. Despite the fact that all of the music is being created by *your* body, you have almost no access to the process that gives rise to it. You glimpse the vast unknowable reality of your body, the incredible complexity of its actions, and the strange fact that it just keeps going. What will be most striking of all will be the even less penetrable idea that what you hear is, for some reason, *beautiful.*

Depending on your beliefs about your nature, this is the moment where you might recognize that God is speaking through you, or that you are channeling a higher power, or that your divine essence is realizing itself. However, the reason that this moment personally fascinates me is that, even from a purely psychological point of view, the awe remains perfectly undiminished. Even the ardent materialist can look down at their body—"a machine made of meat"—and think, "This thing that carries me around all day, that is made of stardust, and grew out of the earth, is able to *make beautiful music… without me!*" ("me," being the part of you that is watching and listening). One reason I am so big on centering the subjective experience of improvisation in my approach to teaching is that that is where you ultimately get to experience what feels like, and might be, *magic*. And the best part is that it will *always* feel like magic. Nothing we learn about the brain will make the *experience* of effortless music-making less awe-inspiring any more than it could make the experience of love less touching or the beauty of art less captivating.

This might be why several students in recent years have told me that learning to improvise on the drums has been *life-*changing. One recently told me that he bursts out laughing with joy when his improvisation is really flowing. Another wrote to say, "[improvisation] has become my form of meditation." If these aren't good enough reasons to patiently develop improvisational fluency on the drums, then perhaps none exist.

Never Stop Playing

Ok, we did it. We spoke about magic in a book about educational theory. Let's gently land back in the world of everyday life by pinpointing a final throughline that drumming offers, from childhood to the grave: if drumming is your hobby of choice, it might be the only form of play you never lose. It is surprising how much you feel like a different person with each decade that passes after childhood. While adult responsibilities pile up, your interest in playful eccentricity diminishes. You start going to bed earlier. You start planning to hang out with people three weeks in advance instead of three hours. You become less willing to sleep on couches and spend nights in airports. I never could have understood this at age sixteen or twenty, but my life was full of opportunities for play, and they would soon begin decreasing.

These changes aren't necessarily regrettable because the meaningfulness of responsibility, commitment, and long-term goals carry a more appropriate weight at this point in life, but I don't think anyone idealizes the goal of living a play-free life of task-fulfillment either. The drums will always be there waiting to be *played*. Remember, to improvise is to be constantly challenged and surprised. Seen in the right light, improvisation is like playing with rhythmic blocks, rearranging them to see if you can build something new without it toppling over, laughing when it becomes a mess, and basking in glory when you finally put the last piece on top and take a step back (perhaps this is the equivalent of smashing Beat 1 on a crash at the end of a particularly challenging combination). The investment of time and energy pays off exponentially because the more proficient an improviser you become, the more blocks you have to play with when you are tinkering away in your drumming sanctuary.

The Sanctuary

When I go to my rehearsal space, I close the door, turn off my phone, and build a wall of sound around me that has much in common with silence. It becomes a sanctuary. In this impenetrable place, it does not feel like I am alone, but like I am with an old friend. My old friend and I know each other better than anyone else could. It is like the best conversation

I have ever had, every time. I am at ease, but engaged. I am challenged, but without self-consciousness. My best ideas appear with this old friend. Sometimes I don't know if the ideas are his or mine, but we feel no need to claim them. We are not concerned with what is said, only with how good it feels to speak.

More than anything else that drumming has given me, I'm grateful that I will always have a place to go where the trivial anxieties of life dissipate, and I can choose to make progress at something I care about, or simply see what my old friend has to say that day.

Resolution

These are some reasons that it might be worth the time to become good at something you care about. If you have chosen the drums, or if the drums have chosen you, you are fortunate to love an instrument that offers so much creative potential. Improvisation is how the instrument becomes an extension of your body. It comes to life and allows you to express things you cannot express without it. Learning to improvise is not easy, but I hope this book has clarified why it need not be as hard as most people think. Why bother? To end by finally addressing the question directly: because it just might be the most rewarding thing you ever learn to do.

Works Cited

1   Dewey, J. (1938). *Experience and education*. Macmillan.

2   James, W. (1918). *The principles of psychology*. H. Holt.

3   Csikszentmihalyi, M. (1990). *Flow: The psychology of optimal experience*. Harper & Row.

4[a-d] Gray, P. O. (2006). *Psychology* (5th). Worth Publishers.

5   Hogarth, R. M. (2001). *Educating intuition*. University of Chicago Press.

6   Carey, B. (2014). *How we learn: The surprising truth about when, where, and why it happens*. Random House.

7   Heerema, E. (2024, August 30). *Using the method of loci for memorization*. Verywell Health. https://www.verywellhealth.com/will-the-method-of-loci-mnemonic-improve-your-memory-98411

8   McNeill, W. H. (1997). *Keeping together in time: Dance and drill in human history*. Harvard University Press.

9   Bellah, R. N. (2011). *Religion in human evolution: From the paleolithic to the axial age*. Belknap Press of Harvard University Press.

10 Winner, E. (2019). *How art works: A psychological exploration*. Oxford University Press.

11 Keltner, D., & Haidt, J. (2003). Approaching awe, a moral, spiritual, and aesthetic emotion. *Cognition & emotion*, 17(2), 297–314. https://doi.org/10.1080/02699930302297

Acknowledgements

First and foremost, I want to thank my editor, publisher, and friend Regina Alvarado. Her feedback made this book better in every way. This project may have never seen the light of day without her going above and beyond at every step. I also want to thank my students. I can only partially claim the ideas in this book because they emerged from our work together. I am continually inspired to become a better teacher thanks to your openness and your trust in me. I want to thank Dr. Patricia Stokes, whom I met while taking her Psychology of Creativity seminar at Columbia University, for making sure my psychology claims were accurate, and for providing a model for everything a university professor should be. I want to thank Amelia Ellis for laying out the book beautifully. Her encouragement made me feel like someone other than me might actually enjoy this book. I want to thank the very busy, sometimes very famous, musicians who made time to read advance copies and offer comments: Steve Vai, John Riley, Matt Halpern, Don Lombardi, Juan Carlito Mendoza, Steve Jocz, Dave DiCenso, and Sergio Bellotti. I want to thank my students and family who proofread advance copies: Iris and Dominique Bouvet, Louise Tuski, Dillon Pinard, Lyam Sharpe, and Tony Pichler. And I want to thank my wife, Kenna, whose loving support, patience, and encouragement is the constant wind in my sails.